Delicious PROBIOTIC DRINKS

75 Recipes for Kombucha, Kefir, Ginger Beer, and Other Naturally Fermented Drinks

JULIA MUELLER

Skyhorse Publishing

10 9 8 7 6 5 4

Library of Congress Cataloging-in-Publication Data is available on file.

Hardcover ISBN: 978-1-62636-392-2
Paperback ISBN: 978-1-5107-5533-8
Ebook ISBN: 978-1-62873-894-0

Printed in China

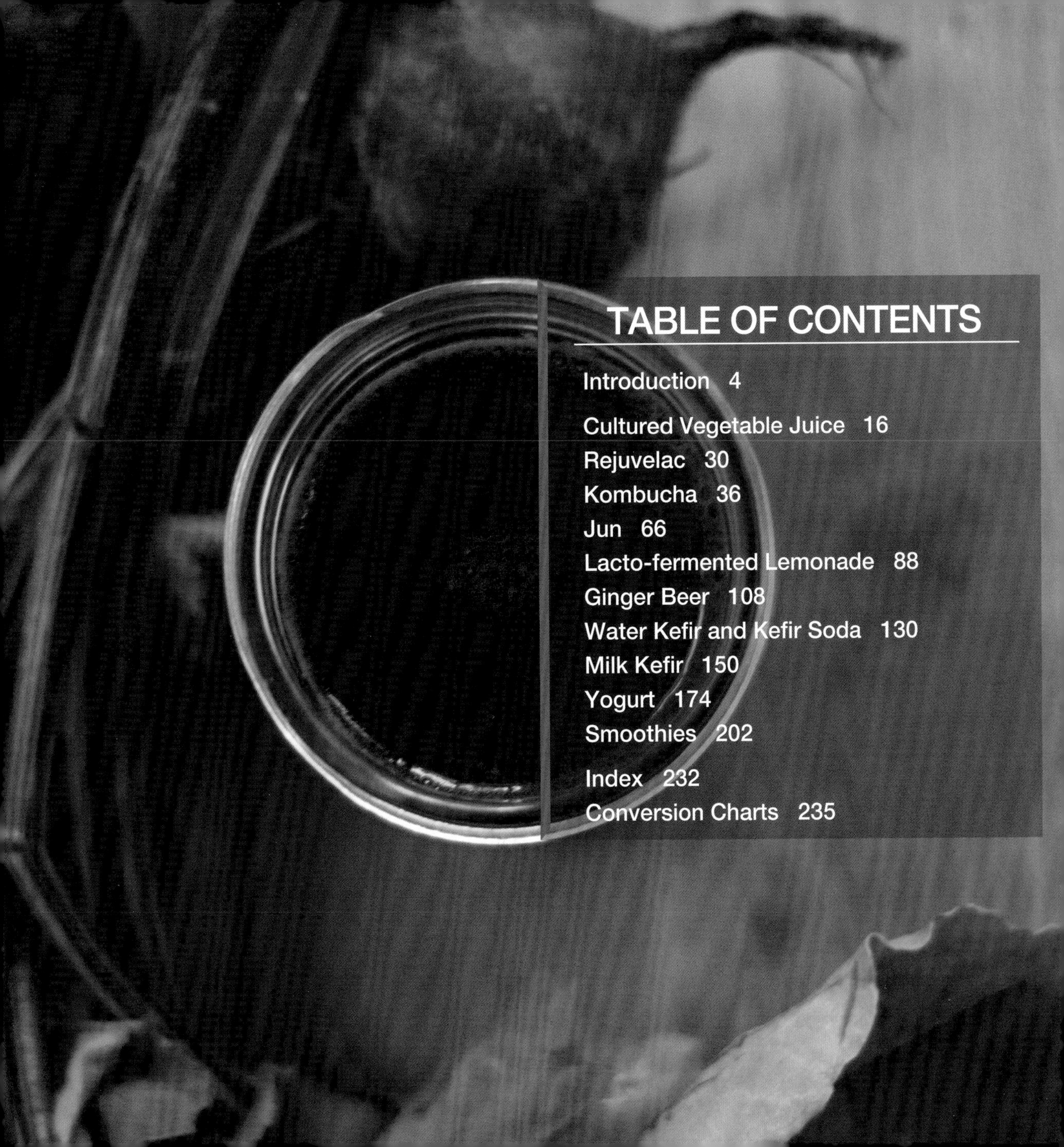

TABLE OF CONTENTS

Introduction

Introduction

Welcome to the wonderful world of probiotic drinks! If you're looking for a fun and delicious way to improve your health, you've come to the right place!

In this book, you will find more than seventy-five recipes for creating ten different types of probiotic beverages. In these pages, you will discover what home brewing is; the health benefits of probiotics and various herbs, fruits, vegetables, and teas; and how to get started making your own delicious probiotic drinks.

The sections in this book are organized by type of beverage. Each section begins with how-to instructions on brewing the drink and then provides recipes for flavoring the beverage to ensure a tasty experience. While this book provides information on fermentation and can act as inspiration for flavor ideas, I welcome you to get creative and cater to your own pallet and nutritional needs, as well as choose techniques that work for you. Remember, fermentation is an art!

Fermentation can be frustrating. It can be time-consuming, confusing, but more than anything, it is absolutely magnificent once you get the hang of it! Not only is the process of fermenting drinks (and food!) fun, but it also teaches you a great deal about basic chemistry and human health—and is utterly delicious.

Fermenting probiotic drinks does not need to be expensive! In fact, it is very cost-effective to brew all of these beverages at home. The internet is a great resource for finding quality probiotic starters, jugs, bottles, jars, and other tools that are necessary for brewing.

Take your time, enjoy the process of growing healthful probiotic cultures, and give yourself a pat on the back for beginning a journey that will affect your health in a very positive way. Remember that there is an ecosystem of organisms inside of you that helps your body with its most basic yet complex functions. Promoting these organisms by establishing a desirable environment for them to thrive will make them healthy and happy, which in turn will do the same for you.

Please be sure to read all of the instructions carefully, as there are some risks involved in fermenting probiotic drinks. Without further adieu, it is time to learn about probiotic beverages!

About Probiotics (and Yeast)

Probiotics are good bacteria that help promote and maintain the microflora in your digestive tract to achieve digestive balance and overall gut health. There are thousands of strains of helpful bacteria and yeast; the type of bacteria touted as being the most beneficial to our digestive systems is Lactobacillius, which is the live culture present in yogurt, kombucha, kefir, ginger beer, etc. While you can purchase a large array of probiotic supplements and drinks from the grocery store, they tend to be pricy and are not always as effective as those made at home.

In the battle of good and evil bacteria, probiotics are the good guys. Probiotics help fight off harmful bacteria, which can prevent or heal sickness, boost immunity, and increase energy. Some companies even manufacture probiotic cleaners for use in your home or commercially to keep a sanitary environment.

On a daily basis, we consume foods lacking in live nutrients. The root of this issue is twofold, beginning with the way our food is sourced and ultimately how our food is prepared. Our meats are often filled with antibiotics and our fresh produce can be genetically modified and sprayed with chemicals. We rely heavily on cooked foods, such as breads and pastas. Because of the convenience of commodity foods, we forget that optimal nutrition comes from a diet rich in raw, whole foods.

While adding probiotic drinks to your diet will not necessarily provide a cure-all for any nutrition deficits, it certainly will help heal your gut from damage that difficult-to-digest foods (such as wheat, beans, legumes, processed sugars) have caused. It will also help establish a positive environment for the existing beneficial microorganisms in your gut to flourish, assisting in the breakdown of food, fighting off pathogens, and boosting your immune system.

Health Benefits of Probiotic Drinks

Each probiotic drink has its own unique strains of bacteria and/or yeasts. There are thousands of strains of helpful bacteria and yeasts, each providing a supportive role in our digestive and immune systems. The health benefits of probiotic drinks are extensive. In each section of this book, I provide a description of the health benefits of the beverage itself as well as the health benefits of the ingredients for each recipe.

Probiotic drinks promote efficient digestion by achieving healthy gut flora, fighting pathogens (thereby promoting immunity), and boosting energy levels for overall vitality. In a sense, fermented foods are "predigested," as sugars in the food or drink have already broken down. This makes them easier to digest than non-fermented foods and creates less work for the pancreas, which is responsible for secreting digestive fluids.

While probiotic drinks have different effects on different people, studies have shown they can help alleviate the following ailments:

- Constipation
- Candida and Leaky Gut Syndrome
- Irritable Bowel Syndrome
- Ulcers
- Yeast Infections
- Celiac Disease
- Crohn's Disease
- Diarrhea
- Diabetes

It is important to keep in mind that while I provide information about the health benefits of each beverage, many in the scientific community still debate to what extent probiotics help us. For this reason, it is important for you to literally follow your gut. Do your own research, and remember these beverages are not a cure-all, nor do they have the same effects on each individual.

About Fermentation

Fermentation is a valuable tool that has been used in various cultures around the world for thousands of years. It has been used for making beer, wine, other fermented beverages, and shelf-stable food, all of which were important to nations prior to refrigeration to ensure a stock of food and drink could be safely kept.

Fermentation is a process that occurs when a live organism grows and multiplies as it eats the food it is supplied and converts it into acid and alcohol. In the case of this cookbook, the live organisms are strains of bacteria and yeast, also known as probiotics. The "food" the probiotics eat comes in a form of sugar: cane sugar, honey, lactose from milk, or fructose from fruit.

Lactic acid, the acid that is produced during fermentation, helps achieve the proper acid balance in your stomach, either by increasing it or lowering it. Having too much or too little stomach acid can be uncomfortable and fermented foods create a balance that is favorable for proper digestion. As people age, the presence of digestive enzymes decline, which is why fermented foods and beverages are particularly useful for older folks.

Another result of fermentation is acetylcholine, which acts as a neurotransmitter in both the peripheral nervous system and the central nervous system. This neurotransmitter is responsible for many complicated functions, such as muscle contraction, maintaining healthy bowel movements, and transmitting information from one side of the brain to the other. Day to day, acetylcholine helps one achieve focus, maintains memory, and calms excitability. In this sense, acetylcholine is vital in learning and retaining information. Studies have shown those with Alzheimer's have lower amounts of acetylcholine, which is why the disease is treated with a synthetic form of the neurotransmitter.

Similar to brewing wine and beer, the sugars present at the beginning of the fermentation are metabolized such that once your drink is brewed, there is much less sugar left than there was when you started. Also similar to wine and beer, most probiotic beverages that are water-based contain a small amount of alcohol. For this reason, it is very important to be cautious when allowing children to drink home-brewed probiotic beverages, especially when the beverages are brewed strong.

In general, depending on the food or beverage, the amount of time and ideal temperature for fermentation varies. For instance, yogurt and kefir take twenty-four hours or less to culture, whereas ginger beer could take a few weeks, and kombucha takes five to seven days. In essence, every bacteria and yeast strain has different needs and the fun and challenging part about growing them is figuring out their ideal environment to end up with a superb beverage.

Secondary Fermentation

While most people are familiar with fermentation, a process known as secondary fermentation is not as widely known. Secondary fermentation is exactly how it sounds: it is a second round of fermentation after the beverage has already undergone a primary fermentation. Secondary fermentation is not a necessary step in brewing probiotic beverages, but it is typically how the beverages get their delicious flavors and effervescence (fizziness). During the first fermentation, most if not all of the sugar is consumed by the probiotics, so additional food (sugar or fruit) is required for the secondary.

What is the purpose of secondary fermentation? For starters, it allows the probiotics to continue to grow so that the beverage becomes even richer in good bacteria. In addition, secondary fermentation is the way most probiotic beverages get flavored. While it is perfectly acceptable and delicious to consume probiotic drinks after they have completed their first fermentation, ingredients such as fruit, sweeteners (sugar or honey), tea, herbs, and/or edible flowers are added prior to fermenting the beverage for the second time, which results in tasty, fun, bubbly drinks adaptable to anyone's taste.

The beverages I love to put through a secondary fermentation are kombucha, jun, ginger beer, and kefir soda. I find secondary fermentation to be unnecessary when it comes to lacto-fermented lemonade, cultured vegetable juice, milk-based kefir, yogurt, and rejuvelac.

Making Probiotic Drinks At Home

Where To Begin

For those who are brand new to fermenting, the process may seem daunting and overwhelming. I assure you, it does not need to be! The best place to start would be to pick a section of this book that interests you. Do you eat yogurt every day and want to try making it on your own? Start with the yogurt or kefir section! Perhaps you've been buying store-bought kombucha and could give your pocket book a break, because—ouch!—kombucha can be expensive. The kombucha or jun section will save you money, give you ultimate control of your flavor preferences, and will give you a healthy project to keep your mind active. Once you choose a drink, you may (or may not) need to make some purchases to ensure you have the proper tools for fermenting.

Fermentation Tools

Each beverage requires some tools that you may already own. After you choose a beverage to ferment, take stock of what you own versus what tools the section calls for. Prior to fermenting the drink, read all of the instructions carefully and make sure you have everything need. Compared to brewing beer or fermenting wine, the equipment you need for the drinks in this book is very inexpensive and can be used for other cooking or storage needs besides fermentation.

In each section, I provide a list of kitchen tools that will be necessary for preparing the beverage. As you gain experience, you will learn which tools work best for you, so you will likely end up adding to and changing your own fermentation tool inventory. In general, you will need a (or several) large glass jug(s), kitchen towels or cheesecloth, stretchy rubber bands, sugar, tea, glass bottles with air-tight lids (both screw-top and flip-cap work!) and access to spring or well water. Spring water can be purchased from the grocery store in large jugs, which is the best option for fermenting probiotic beverages unless your house runs on a well. To make your fermenting experience even more cost effective, become a savvy bargain shopper by comparing prices on jugs, bottles, or jars in big box stores versus online stores.

While all of the drinks in this book can be enjoyed in their original form, livening them up with your favorite flavors adds a unique, artisanal quality to your craft beverages and makes them taste amazing! The combination of various fruits, herbs, spices, tea, flowers, and sweeteners allows for virtually endless options.

In each section, I provide recipes that add flavor to your homemade probiotic beverages. It is important to remember that the sweetness, strength, and length of time of the beverage prior to flavoring affects how it tastes once you add ingredients. For this reason, feel free to add and subtract according to your personal preferences. Unless otherwise noted, I recommend using fresh, in-season produce for every recipe in this book. Below is a list of fruit by season.

Winter	December, January, February	clementines, dates, grapefruit, kiwifruit, oranges, passion fruit, pear, persimmons, red currants, tangerines
Spring	March, April, May	apricots, cherimoya, cherries, honeydew, jackfruit, limes, lychee, mango, oranges, pineapple, strawberries
Summer	June, July, August	apricots, black currants, blackberries, blueberries, boysenberries, cantaloupe, cherries, durian, elderberries, figs, grapefruit, grapes, honeydew, jackfruit, key limes, lychee, mulberries, nectarines, passion fruit, peaches, plums, raspberries, strawberries, watermelon
Fall	September, October, November	apples, cranberries, grapes, guava, huckleberries, key limes, kumquat, passion fruit, pears, persimmons, pineapple, pomegranate
Fruit that is great year round: apples, avocado, bananas, coconut, lemons		

> *"Note that 100 percent pure fruit juices can be used for the secondary fermentation of any water-based beverages in this book. While fruit juice is a quick, easy, and affordable way of flavoring drinks, juices are highly concentrated in sugar and do not provide the same health benefits as fresh fruit. In addition, I have found that leaving fruit pulp inside the bottles while a beverage is undergoing secondary fermentation helps the beverage become fizzy. It is more difficult to achieve a bubbly drink when using store-bought fruit juice for secondary fermentation."*

Helpful Liquid Conversions:

1 liter	4.2 cups
16 ounces	2 cups
1 gallon	3.78 liters = 16 cups

Brewing To Perfection

It can be difficult to achieve the exact same results every time you brew probiotic beverages. You may use the same exact ingredients for secondary fermentation, but the flavor may change from one batch to the next due to temperature maintenance, the amount of sugar already present versus amount of added sugar, the maturity of the culture, etc. All of these factors play a cause-and-effect role in the outcome of the beverage. On the following pages, I list specific flavors you experience when drinking fermented beverages and discuss how those flavors are achieved so that you can change or maintain your brewing methods according to taste.

Dry: When a drink tastes dry (not sweet), the sugars have been metabolized by the culture, resulting in low residual sugar. Some people prefer dry beverages, while others like their drinks to be sweeter. To avoid a dry beverage, carefully monitor the brewing process by tasting the drink throughout primary or secondary fermentation to ensure the sweetness is where you want it to be. To check sweetness during primary fermentation, spoon out some of the liquid using a sanitized spoon or a small glass. During secondary fermentation, you can open a bottle after twenty-four hours to see if it is at the sweetness level you like. Once a beverage is at the desired level of sweetness, simply stop the brewing process by bottling and refrigerating the drink.

Sweet: All beverages in this book contain sugars, whether they are naturally occurring (such as the lactose in milk or the carbohydrates in vegetables) or added for fermentation. Once a beverage is finished fermenting, much of the sugar will have been eaten, causing it to be less sweet than when fermentation began.

If a drink tastes sweet at the end of fermentation, it is because the probiotics and yeasts did not consume all of the sugars, which means it can ferment longer if desired. For those who prefer sweeter drinks, you can add additional sugars, such as cane sugar, honey, or fruit, to sweeten the beverage, but this should be done after the primary fermentation is over, as too much sugar at the onset of fermentation can kill the cultures.

Tart: Certain beverages such as kombucha, kefir, and cultured vegetable juice have a tart element to them, which is a flavor by product of fermentation. Do not mistake a tart flavor for spoilage, because many of the beverages in this book, when fermented correctly, should taste tart when they are finished fermenting. The stronger a beverage is, the more tart it is.

To achieve a beverage that is more tart, brew the beverage longer, but be mindful of the brew time, as you can starve the probiotics if they do not have enough sugar to eat. Also pay attention to the pH level of the beverage, as a pH that is too acidic can be harmful to your digestive system.

Creamy: Creaminess is typically associated with dairy products, so it is only natural that kefir and yogurt should have a creamy flavor and texture; however, there are other beverages that have a somewhat creamy taste and mouthfeel. Ginger beer, for instance, can have a creamy flavor when it is not overly dry (meaning the ginger beer is still sweet and the probiotics have not consumed all the sugars). Jun can also taste creamy because of the flavor the probiotics yield after consuming the honey.

Yeasty/Lemony: Most beverages in this book will have a very subtle lemon and/or yeast flavor, which is a definite sign of fermentation because it signifies the presence of yeast. Yeasts that occur in probiotic drinks act similarly to bread yeasts. They feed off of sugars, grow, and they even taste similar to bread yeasts. Yeast and lemon flavors are most detectable in rejuvelac, water kefir (or kefir soda), cultured vegetable juice, and ginger beer, but even milk-based kefir and other beverages can taste slightly yeasty.

Effervescent: When discussing fermentation and natural carbonation, the term commonly used is "effervescent." All beverages in this book are effervescent (including milk-based kefir and yogurt!), albeit some more than others. Kombucha, kefir soda, and ginger beer are the most effervescent drinks and can be just as fizzy as soda.

Effervescence is typically achieved during secondary fermentation when additional sugars have been added and the liquid has been sealed in air-tight bottles. The bacteria and yeast put off gases that build when bottled and this pressure results in natural carbonation. Do not be surprised if cultured vegetable juice, rejuvelac, and lacto-fermented lemonade become slightly fizzy, as this is a normal product of fermentation.

It is very important to be mindful of drinks in sealed glass bottles for secondary fermentation. The longer the liquid ferments, the more effervescent the beverage becomes, which means bottles can explode if the drinks are left to ferment for too long. Also bear in mind that while refrigeration slows the fermentation process, it does not stop it, so probiotic drinks will continue to ferment and become fizzy in the refrigerator. When achieving your desired level of fizz, the trick is to allow just enough secondary fermentation time for the drink to begin carbonating and then refrigerate it for a couple of days prior to drinking it. This allows the drink to continue to ferment but not to the extent that it will be too pressurized.

Cautionary Notes:

Making any fermented beverage at home can be risky. Provided you follow the instructions outlined in this book and pay attention to your probiotics, you will not only brew delicious probiotic drinks, but you will have the satisfaction of knowing that you made something really cool (and healthy) at home! Each section of this book indicates the risks associated with preparing the beverage and explains how to avoid error.

Sanitation

It is important to be mindful of keeping everything you use for fermenting probiotic beverages sanitized. Giving the probiotics a healthful environment will not only ensure their survival, but will also help you avoid contamination and achieve a superior product. Be sure to read the instructions provided in each section carefully and trust your instincts.

When fermenting more than one probiotic drink at a time . . .

You may become ambitious and decide to make several types of probiotic beverages at once. Chances are you will have jars and jugs strewn helter skelter all over your house. Be sure to keep different types of fermented beverages as far apart as possible (fifteen feet apart at the very least). Strains of probiotics do become airborne during the fermentation process and, if a strain from one fermenting beverage lands on another one, it can change the culture and morph into something completely different. To maintain purity in your cultures, keep them away from one another.

If you do ferment more than one type of probiotic beverage at a time, I strongly recommend using a notepad or spreadsheet to track what day you started brewing which beverage. This way, you can use it as reference if you lose track of how long a specific beverage has been brewing. Length of time is crucial when it comes to brewing, so be aware of what stage all your beverages are at in the fermentation process.

Cultured
Vegetable Juice

About Cultured Vegetable Juice

While sweet, fruity probiotic drinks illicit greater excitement than fermented vegetable juice, the recipes in this section are so packed with nutrients and probiotics, they trump any fruit-filled probiotic drink around. For the most cleansing, vitamin- and mineral-filled, antioxidant-rich beverages, this is the section to consult!

Other cultures, particularly Eastern Europe and India, are much more receptive to salty, sour, fermented vegetable juices. Records from hundreds of years ago state that drinks such as beet kvass were safer to drink than plain water because the probiotics fought off bad bacteria and pathogens present in contaminated water.

Recently, there has been a great deal of excitement about fermented foods—and for a very good reason. When vegetables are fermented, the natural sugars are consumed by probiotics and converted into carbon dioxide and organic acids. This process results in vegetables considered to be "predigested," meaning the probiotics have helped break down the carbohydrates, making the vegetables easier to digest. The liquid surrounding the fermented vegetables is also full of enzymes and nutrients and helps our digestive systems break down food while easing any digestive discomfort.

Fermenting vegetables is very easy. All the process requires is a selection of raw chopped vegetables, water, and salt. From there, one can add various spices and herbs and/or culture starters such as whey, kefir starter, or cultured vegetable juice starter. Whey can be obtained by straining yogurt using cheesecloth (for more detailed instructions, see the section on Lacto-Fermented Lemonade), and freeze-dried starters are available to purchase at natural food stores or over the Internet. In general, 1 cup of whey or 1 packet of freeze-dried starter (roughly 5 grams) per 1 gallon of liquid is sufficient for fermenting.

Keep in mind, there are a myriad variations of cultured vegetable juice that can be made, leaving room to choose vegetables based on personal taste and dietary needs. Choosing starchy vegetables, or vegetables with high sugar content, yields the best results because they provide ample food for the yeasts and probiotics to feed off of. Vegetables such as cabbage, beets, carrots, cucumbers, squash, radishes, ginger, onions, garlic, and cauliflower work well for pickling and for making fermented vegetable juice. Adding sea salt, black or white peppercorns, fresh dill or other herbs, ground mustard, chili powder, or other spices, helps generate a flavor that you can enjoy.

Keep in mind, there are myriad variations of cultured vegetable juice that can be made, leaving room to choose vegetables based on personal taste and dietary needs. Choosing starchy vegetables, or vegetables with high sugar content, yields the best results because they provide ample food for the yeasts and probiotics to feed off. Vegetables such as cabbage, beets, carrots, cucumbers, squash, radishes, ginger, onions, garlic, and cauliflower work well for pickling and for making fermented vegetable juice. Adding sea salt, black or white peppercorns, fresh dill or other herbs, ground mustard, chili powder, or other spices helps generate a flavor that you can enjoy.

While fermented foods available for purchase at the grocery store are still tasty and somewhat nutritious, they not only contain less nutrient density than those made at home, but it is also difficult to find a product that contains active cultures, as it is industry standard to pasteurize most food. Heating cultured vegetables or vegetable juice kills the lactobacilli and also dissolves the enzymes, rendering the drink inactive from a probiotic standpoint. In this sense, one can enjoy store-bought sauerkraut or pickles for taste and a small amount of health benefits, but drinking the juice surrounding the vegetables is not necessarily going to provide the same digestive aid as making it homemade.

Health Benefits of Cultured Vegetable Juice

Have you ever known a friend or family member who drinks pickle juice? While this urge may seem gross to some, it comes quite naturally to others. These cravings can be the result of your body seeking one or many of the numerous health benefits of fermented juice. Taking into perspective the density of nourishment, it is easy to see why one would be dying for pickle juice or a sausage with sauerkraut. It all makes sense, because fermented foods and vegetable juice are incredibly . . .

1. Hydrating: cultured vegetable juice contains electrolytes (potassium, magnesium, sodium, etc), which quenches thirst and hydrates better than water. While electrolyte sport drinks are popular to drink during exercise, imagine how much more nourishing a glass of cultured vegetable juice is over the sugar-filled store-bought drinks!

2. Helpful to maintain a happy digestive system: cultured veggie juice is full of live probiotics, yeasts, and enzymes, which establish and promote healthy digestive bacteria, assist in the breakdown of food, and ensure proper nutrient absorption.

3. *Rich in vitamins and minerals:* during the fermentation process, the vitamins and minerals in the vegetables are infused into the liquid, providing a nourishing elixir.

4. *Effective for treating various disorders, diseases, and infections:* the nutrients and probiotics in raw cultured vegetable juice have been known to treat digestive problems relating to overgrowth (or even undergrowth) of yeasts, such as candida, vaginal yeast infections, ulcers, and constipation.

5. *Delicious! Okay,* so cultured vegetable juice may be an acquired taste, but give it time and you may find yourself craving the zesty flavors!

Temperature and Time

The cooler your house, the slower the fermentation time of cultured vegetable juice. During the summer, fermentation requires less time, so it is important to pay attention to the progress of the beverage. The time it takes to ferment vegetable juice decreases when a starter is added to the recipe. If no starter is added, fermentation time requires at least four days and can go longer depending on the beverage strength you are looking for.

Cabbage and Carrot Probiotic Juice

There are naturally occurring yeasts and microbes in fresh vegetables, which grow and produce probiotics when they are fermented. One can ferment virtually any vegetable, but those with high amounts of sugars and carbohydrates tend to yield the best fermented results. Chopping up fresh vegetables such as cabbage, carrots, beets, ginger, squash, celery, cucumbers, garlic, or cauliflower and fermenting them in a brine results in a beverage full of vitamins and minerals and digestive health benefits.

While this recipe provides specific ingredients for a cultured vegetable juice, use a combination of any vegetables you like to meet your nutritional needs and desires. The cabbage, carrots, and ginger in this recipe make for a drink that is very soothing for the digestive system, easy to ferment, and is a great introduction to fermented vegetable juices for those not accustomed to them.

Ingredients:

- ½ head cabbage, sliced
- 3 carrots, grated
- 1 tablespoon ginger, grated
- 2 teaspoons sea salt
- Well or spring water for soaking vegetables

You also need:

- 2-quart sized jar
- Cheesecloth or kitchen towel
- Rubber band
- Long handle spoon for stirring

Instructions:

1. Place the cabbage, carrots, ginger, and sea salt in a 2-quart sized jar.
2. Fill the jar with spring or well water.
3. Place cheesecloth or a kitchen towel over the jar and secure it with a rubber band to keep the bugs out.

4. Leave jar in a warm, dark place for four to six days, stirring well twice a day. Bubbles and grayish foam will form on the surface of the liquid, which is completely normal and should not be interpreted as spoilage. When the juice is finished, it will smell somewhat sour, yeasty, and vinegary (not rotten).

5. Strain the juice off of the vegetables and either drink immediately or pour into a sealable jar or bottle and keep in the refrigerator for up to one week.

Note:
You may make a second batch of cultured vegetable juice using the same vegetables, although the second batch will be slightly weaker and will take closer to six days to ferment. As an alternative, you can eat the pickled vegetables, which are delicious and also great for you.

Beet Kvass

Beet Kvass is a highly nutrient-dense probiotic drink made from fermenting beets. This drink is typically made and consumed in Russia and Eastern European countries. Because of its sour, salty, earthy flavor, it is not popular in the United States, as we are accustomed to our beverages being sweet instead of savory. Kvass is traditionally made using stale bread, raisins and other dried fruits, and a vegetable culture starter, but beet kvass can be made with just beets, water, and salt. Or the fermentation can be helped along by adding a culture starter such as whey, freeze-dried kefir starter, or freeze-dried vegetable culture starter. These starters help speed the fermentation and also dramatically lower the amount of salt required.

This cultured beverage could arguably be the most nutrient-dense and beneficial drink in this whole book due to the vitamin and mineral density of beets, on top of the probiotic quality. Beets are full of antioxidants, help detox your blood, and can slow the growth of cancer or tumor cells. They also contain folate, manganese, potassium, fiber, and vitamin C.

As if beets weren't great enough for you as is, their health benefits are enhanced by fermentation. Beet kvass helps clean the liver, creates digestive regularity, can be used to treat kidney stones, and is even more hydrating than water. The betacyanin in beets increases the amount of oxygen that blood cells can carry and is known for purifying the blood.

If the sour flavor of beet kvass is not palatable, worry not. It is an acquired taste and you can use it for soup, bloody marys (or other vegetable cocktails), or add to salad dressing while your taste buds grow accustomed to it.

Ingredients:

- large beet, diced into ½" pieces (about 3 cups worth)
- tablespoon sea salt
- 2 quarts spring or well water

You also need:

- 1 quart-sized jar
- Cheesecloth or kitchen towel
- Rubber band
- Long handle spoon for stirring

Instructions:

1. Scrub the beet well and chop it into ½" pieces. You can also slice the beets—you simply want to be sure each piece has a decent amount of surface area.

2. Add the chopped beets and sea salt to a 2-quart sized jar.

3. Fill the jar with spring or well water and then cover it with cheesecloth or a kitchen towel. Secure the towel with a rubber band.

4. Leave the jar on the counter or in a pantry for a minimum of four days and up to two weeks, stirring frequently. If you allow this beverage to ferment for more than a few days, mold will form on the surface. This is normal. The mold can be scooped off and the liquid can be strained and consumed. For those who are new to beet kvass, ferment the beverage for only a few days to start out, working your way up to a longer fermentation time for the next batch. The liquid will smell sour and should taste sour more than salty. The liquid may also carry a yeasty effervescence and get a little foamy. The gray foam that forms on top is not an indicator that the drink has gone bad. Simply scoop it off, stir the mixture, and continue allowing the beverage to ferment until it tastes sour and slightly effervescent.

5. When ready to drink, strain the liquid from the beets. You can add other juices to the beet juice or dilute it with water if that is your preference.

Kanji

One of the most popular cultured vegetable juices consumed worldwide is kanji. Kanji is typically made by fermenting carrots (particularly purple carrots) with various pickling spices and can also be made with other vegetables such as beets. The jar of pickling vegetables is left in direct sunlight for a few days, during which time the natural enzymes, yeasts, and microbes in the vegetables are released and multiply.

Kanji originates from and is most popular in the northern part of India, where sour, salty drinks are commonplace. This deep purple beverage tends to be served as an appetizer or alongside a meal. Just like the other beverages in this book, there is an abundance of probiotics in kanji, which helps maintain healthy gut flora for regular digestion and nutrient absorption, allowing the body to more efficiently process foods that are normally difficult to digest. On top of the probiotics, this kanji is rich in minerals and vitamins.

Ingredients:

- 2 medium-sized red beets
- 6 medium-sized carrots
- 2½ tablespoons mustard powder (or fresh ground mustard seed)
- 1 teaspoons chili powder
- 8 cups lukewarm water (filtered or well water recommended)

You also need:

- 1 quart-sized jar
- Cheesecloth or kitchen towel
- Rubber band
- Long handle spoon for stirring

Instructions:

1. Wash and peel the vegetables. Chop them into thick strips (french-fry shapes) to maximize surface area and place them in a glass jar or jug.

2. Add the ground mustard and chili powder to a large jar or jug.

3. Pour the lukewarm (filtered) water in the jar and mix until the mustard and chili powder is dissolved and incorporated.

4. Add the chopped beets and carrots.

5. Cover with a lid or cheesecloth fastened with a rubber band.

6. Place jar on a window sill or well-lit area in direct sunlight.

7. Allow the jar to sit for two to three days to ferment, stirring once or twice a day with a clean wooden spoon.

8. Once the kanji tastes sour, small bubbles rise from the bottom to the top of the jar, and a bubbly foam forms at the top, the beverage is ready. This process should take no longer than three days in a warm house, and up to five in a cooler house.

9. Strain the liquid into a glass or bottles, saving the beets and carrots to eat if desired.

10. Refrigerate kanji and serve immediately or save in sealed bottles for up to one week.

Note:
You can eat the pickled beets and carrots or use them for a second batch of kanji, although the second batch will take slightly longer to ferment.

Rejuvelac

About Rejuvelac

Rejuvelac is the liquid strained off sprouted grains. When sprouted grains soak in water and ferment, the naturally occurring microorganisms inside of the grains and yeast in the air grow into the probiotic beverage known as rejuvelac. Rejuvelac is one of the fastest-fermenting probiotic beverages. The whole process can be completed in three days. For this reason, it is important to pay attention to the rejuvelac while it is fermenting—it doesn't take much time for a batch to go bad if it sits for too long. Rye is the most popular grain for making rejuvelac because of its favorable taste over other grains. The best grains for making rejuvelac are buckwheat grouts, wheat berries, oats, barley, quinoa, and rice.

While rejuvelac carries the same digestive benefits as any other probiotic drink in this book, it is an acquired taste. The flavor is subtle, slightly yeasty, and slightly lemony. Drinking this beverage with fresh lemon juice or mixed with 100 percent juices is the way most people prefer it. You can also add it to smoothies or even use it for vegan cooking.

Rejuvelac and Vegan Food:

While rejuvelac is great for drinking plain, it can also be used as a starter to ferment vegan nut cheeses, yogurt, and sauces. An easy recipe for vegan nut cheese involves little more than raw cashews and a small amount of rejuvelac. One can even mimic cream cheese for creating baked vegan desserts using rejuvelac.

TROUBLESHOOTING:

It should only take a couple of days for the grains to sprout. If it takes longer, it could be that the grains you are using have been toasted or heat treated such that they are not able to sprout. It is best to source your grains that are specific for sprouting. You can find these at a natural food store or over the Internet.

Basic Rejuvelac

Ingredients:

- 1 cup rye grains*
- 1 quart spring or well water

**Also try buckwheat grouts, wheat berries, oats, barley, quinoa, or rice*

You also need:

- 1 quart-sized jar
- Cheesecloth, kitchen towel, or sprouting screw top
- Rubber band

Instructions:

1. Pour the grains into the jar and fill the jar with water. Stir the grains.
2. Cover the jar with cheesecloth or a kitchen towel secured by a rubber band (or screw a sprouting top on the jar). Leave jar at room temperature (70°F works best) in a dark place overnight (up to twelve hours).
3. Strain the water off of the grains and rinse the grains well until the water that comes off them is completely clear and no longer appears brown or murky. Toss the grains around in the strainer to try to get all of the water off—you don't want excess water on the grains when you put them back into the jar.
4. Place the grains back into the jar and cover. Leave the jar at in a dark place again.
5. Every eight hours, rinse the grains well and place them back in the jar with as little excess water as possible. Repeat this process until the grains sprout—small tails will poke out of the grains. In a warm house, this process should take one-and-a-half to two days. In a cooler house, it could take up to three.
6. Once the grains have sprouted, fill the jar with 4 cups of water, cover it with cheesecloth bound by a rubber band (or a sprouting lid), and leave in a dark place for 2 days.
7. The liquid is the rejuvelac and should smell somewhat yeasty (not foul!) and lemony. The liquid will be mostly transparent but somewhat cloudy. There will be tiny bubbles that rush from the bottom of the jar (where the grains are) to the surface. This is an indication of fermentation.
8. Most people prefer their rejuvelac cold, so refrigerate the liquid prior to drinking.
9. You can now use the same grains to make one more batch of rejuvelac. The second batch will only take one day to ferment.

Rejuvelac & Juice

Rejuvelac can be a bit of an acquired taste for a lot of people. The flavor can be slightly yeasty and lemony and can require some getting used to. For those who do not enjoy the flavor of rejuvelac, there are definitely flavor options! Simply add 1 cup of 100 percent juice for every 1 cup of rejuvelac and enjoy a great taste plus added health benefits. You can also add a squeeze of lemon to the rejuvelac for a refreshing beverage!

Ingredients

- 1 cup rejuvelac (page 33)
- 1 cup 100% juice, such as cranberry (as seen in photo), pomegranate, apple, blueberry

Instructions:

In a large glass or pitcher, pour both the rejuvelac and the juice, stir together and serve!

Kombucha

About Kombucha

Kombucha is a naturally bubbly (or "effervescent") probiotic drink. It originated in Northeast China then made its way to Russia. Kombucha was then brought to Germany, followed by the rest of Europe and the world. Kombucha is made from a living organism called a SCOBY, which stands for Symbiotic Culture of Bacteria and Yeast. A SCOBY is often referred to as a "mushroom" or "the mother." It grows, multiplies, ferments, and feeds off tea and sugar. The probiotics and yeast eat the sugar, which ferments the beverage and results in a drink that is acidic, probiotic-rich, and mildly alcoholic. Just like all recipes in this book, it is important to take precautions when fermenting living organisms.

Kombucha contains acetic acid, which is a mild natural antibiotic. Because of the acidity of kombucha, bad strains of bacteria cannot grow in the culture, as the environment is not optimal for survival or reproduction. In this way, the good bacteria thrive while the bad bacteria have no fighting chance. Kombucha also contains lactic acid, and is rich in B vitamins, folate, and antioxidants.

It is stated that kombucha can aid in digestion, increase energy, manage hunger, and can create pH balance in the digestive tract. There is still a great deal of debate on whether there is scientific proof to support these health claims. It is important to keep in mind that this book makes no claim that kombucha will improve health nor will the alleged benefits apply to all individuals. Regardless, kombucha tastes great and most people report that it gives their digestive system regularity and makes them feel good.

If you have purchased kombucha or any other form of probiotic beverage from the grocery store, you have no doubt noticed how expensive it is. I began brewing kombucha because I was drinking store-bought kombucha every day and the cost was becoming unreasonable for my budget. With a few small start-up costs, I began brewing kombucha, which is an investment that has paid for itself hundreds of times over.

Brewing kombucha may seem very daunting and intimidating at first, but don't let the long list of instructions fool you. It's actually very easy to make homemade kombucha, but I want to emphasize the importance of brewing safely by providing detailed instructions.

How to Start

To brew kombucha, you need several kitchen tools plus a kombucha SCOBY in starter liquid. Starter liquid is simply unflavored homebrewed kombucha. There are many online sources from which you can purchase a SCOBY. I caution you to read reviews and talk to others who have purchased from the specific suppliers you are looking at because the quality of some SCOBY suppliers is more reliable than others. If you do choose to purchase your SCOBY online, make sure you begin brewing as soon as possible because the SCOBY will already be in slight shock from traveling and it is important to get it fed and in a healthy environment.

Keeping Your SCOBY and Kombucha Healthy

What does it mean to keep a SCOBY healthy? I will touch on this throughout the list of instructions, but essentially it means the following:

1. Feeding the SCOBY a mixture of tea and sugar; 100 percent black tea works best for brewing kombucha, but you may also use 100 percent green tea. Fancy teas typically contain peels and other ingredients that are not conducive to brewing kombucha. Plain black tea works great.

2. Keeping it out of the sunlight in a dark place: a closet shelf works as an excellent home for brewing kombucha or jun.

3. Keeping it covered while still allowing it to breathe: a kitchen towel or cheesecloth secured by a stretchy rubber band works perfectly to keep out the bugs.

4. Giving it an optimal temperature range (between 75° and 85° Fahrenheit).

5. Keeping the SCOBY moist with starter liquid. I recommend maintaining at least two inches of starter liquid for every one inch of SCOBY.

If you choose to purchase your SCOBY online, make sure you begin brewing a batch as soon as you receive it, as the SCOBY will be in shock.

Giving One of Your SCOBYs Away

With each new batch of kombucha you brew, a new SCOBY will form. While it is perfectly okay to allow the SCOBY to continue to grow, I find my SCOBY looks healthiest when it is three inches thick or less. You can peel off layers of your kombucha SCOBY and give them to your friends or family.

To do so, add starter liquid (which is simply kombucha) and a SCOBY to a plastic bag. Seal well and make sure the SCOBY lays flat and is out of direct sunlight while it is transported.

Because the SCOBY will be in shock from traveling, it is important to remove it from the bag as soon as possible so it can breathe. Inform the person you give the SCOBY to that they should brew a batch of kombucha as soon as they get the SCOBY home.

Fermenting Kombucha

Like any fermentation process, there needs to be food for the active probiotics and yeasts to feed off. For kombucha, food is tea and sugar. Each batch of kombucha you brew, a new SCOBY will form and the SCOBY will grow to the width of the container it is in. For instance, once you are on your fifth batch of kombucha, you will have five layers of SCOBY. As you brew, you can allow your SCOBY to grow, and you don't need to discard it until it reaches more than three inches thick.

In addition to tea and sugar, kombucha requires an optimal temperature range to flourish. Between 75° and 85° Fahrenheit is the optimal temperature range for brewing kombucha. While it is generally okay for kombucha to experience temperatures outside that range, you will notice a difference in the strength of the kombucha if it is brewing below 70° or above 80°. A lower temperature may require a longer brewing time, whereas a higher temperature will make the fermentation process go faster. Too warm a temperature can kill the probiotics.

The fun part about brewing kombucha is flavoring it. It is perfectly fine to drink the kombucha you brew plain and not put it through a secondary fermentation; however, for the purpose of your kombucha enjoyment, I have included multiple recipes that you can use to make fizzy, sweet kombucha that can be enjoyed throughout the year. Note that kombucha should be flavored after it has gone through the first fermentation, as putting anything other than sweetened tea in a SCOBY's environment can change the structure and health of the probiotics.

What is Secondary Fermentation and How Does it Work?

Secondary fermentation involves fermenting a beverage that has already been fermented for a second time. When you brew kombucha for the first fermentation, the bacteria and yeast feed off the sugar and tea that you give them. Once all of the "food" has been consumed by the probiotics, they are ready for more. This is where secondary fermentation comes in.

Immediately after the first fermentation (before you refrigerate the kombucha), you can add additional tea and water to begin a secondary fermentation. You can also add various fruits, herbs, and non-toxic flowers to flavor your kombucha to your liking. Once you have added additional ingredients, you can then bottle the kombucha and leave it in a dark place at room temperature for two to three days and the kombucha will continue fermenting.

Since the bottles are sealed, some pressure will build and the beverage will then become effervescent (or naturally carbonated). Similar to the first fermentation, the more sugar you add, the longer it will take the probiotics to process it. If you want your kombucha sweet, you can either add more sugar (cane sugar or fruit) than necessary or only allow the second fermentation to last one or two days versus two to three. Fermentation slows when you refrigerate the kombucha but does not stop completely.

Now here comes the really cool part! Depending on what you use for the secondary fermentation, you will end up with varying levels of effervescence. I found that more acidic fruit yields a more effervescent kombucha. I have also found that leaving fruit pulp inside the bottles during the secondary fermentation results in more effervescence. Additionally, allowing the sealed bottles to refrigerate for at least twenty-four hours before popping the bottle open will yield a more effervescent kombucha.

To summarize: to get the most effervescent kombucha (if that is what you're going for), use an acidic fruit for the secondary fermentation process, leaving the pulp inside the bottles and allowing the bottles to sit for two to three days at room temperature. Then refrigerate the bottles for one to two days before drinking. Berries, apricots, and pineapple have resulted in the spunkiest kombucha in my experience. Remember to shorten the length of the secondary fermentation if you desire a sweeter (less dry) kombucha.

Because pressure and effervescence builds during the secondary fermentation, it is very important that you point the bottles away from your face when you open them. If you are using good quality flip-cap bottles, it is likely that you will have a batch or two of kombucha that will fizz out of the bottle when opened, similar to opening a can of soda after it's been rolling around in the back of your car). Just be sure to open the bottles over the sink and never point them at your face or anything breakable. Do not ever give a small child a bottle of kombucha to open.

Kombucha and Allergies and/or Detox

A very small portion of the population is allergic to kombucha. The exact science behind the allergy is unknown. Similar to doing a juice cleanse, some people go through a detoxification after drinking kombucha. This may be perceived as an allergic reaction but it could be the body ridding itself of toxins. Symptoms of detox include headache, more frequent than usual bowel movements, runny nose, or even vomiting. Should you experience any of these symptoms, it is best to consult a doctor before attempting to consume any more kombucha.

It is not recommended to drink homemade kombucha on an empty stomach. If your stomach ever hurts after drinking kombucha, it could mean one of three things—your batch is bad (unlikely, unless you notice mold and/or the batch tastes abnormal), you drank too much, or your kombucha is too strong. Depending on the ingredients added for secondary fermentation, it is possible for people to have a negative reaction to one flavor and have no problem with other flavors.

Taking a Break Between Batches of Kombucha

By no means do you have to continue brewing kombucha forever and ever with no break between batches. Once your SCOBY is growing, you may consider peeling off one of the SCOBYs and using it in an additional jug to brew a higher volume of kombucha at one time. With that said, you may end up with more kombucha than you feel you need or you may simply get sick of brewing. Never fear, you don't have to throw your kombucha SCOBY out! You can store your kombucha SCOBY in the same way you would store kombucha that is brewing: in a jar covered with cheesecloth bound with a rubber band.

Be sure there is plenty of starter fluid to keep the SCOBY moist. One inch of starter fluid for every one inch of SCOBY works well. You will need this starter fluid to keep your SCOBY alive and also to start your next batch when you are ready to brew again. If you go several weeks between batches, check on the SCOBY every once in a while to be sure it still has ample starter fluid.

Cleaning Your Tools

It is very important that everything you use that touches the SCOBY and/or kombucha be properly sanitized. You can sanitize your tools in the dishwasher, or with hot, soapy water, or by soaking them in distilled white vinegar for a couple minutes. If there is harmful bacteria on any of the tools you use, it can potentially contaminate your kombucha.

You do not need to clean the jug that you use to brew kombucha between batches. I do, however, recommend that you clean it periodically (I clean mine every three to five batches). To clean the jug, pour all of the kombucha liquid into bottles (if you haven't already) except for a small amount of fluid to act as starter for your next batch. Place the SCOBY and starter fluid into a glass or stainless steel bowl and cover with a kitchen towel. Fill the jug with very hot, soapy water and use a sponge to get every last bit of kombucha culture out. I repeat this process multiple times to ensure my jug is sanitary.

Distilled white vinegar acts as a sanitizing agent, so you can use vinegar to clean the jug, as well. Pour about ½ cup of distilled white vinegar in the jug and slosh it around for a minute or two. Pour the vinegar out. You can either rinse the jug with clean spring/well water or simply leave it as is. A little bit of residual vinegar will not harm your SCOBY.

Now you can start another batch of kombucha by first adding your tea/sugar mixture to the jug and then carefully (and with clean hands) pouring the starter liquid and SCOBY back in the jug. Secure the opening with cheesecloth bound by a rubber band.

Flavoring Your Kombucha

While it is not necessary to add flavors to kombucha once it has finished its primary fermentation, experimenting with flavors is by far the most fun part of brewing kombucha! There are a myriad of options for giving your kombucha flavor, spunk, and fizz. Fresh fruit and herbs are my favorite ingredients to add before secondary fermentation to ensure the beverage will be bubbly, just the right amount of sweetness, and full of added health benefits.

One-hundred percent fruit juices are also effective for secondary fermentation, although not to the same extent as fresh fruit. Kombucha likes fruit pulp and tends to be much fizzier when fruit pulp is added for secondary fermentation. For every one gallon of kombucha, 1 cup of fruit juice can be added for secondary fermentation.

It is important to be mindful of the strength of your kombucha. If your kombucha is strong (meaning its pH is lower than 2.5), dilute it with additional sweetened tea along with fruit or other ingredients prior to the secondary fermentation. This ensures there will be enough sugar and tea for the probiotics to feed on for an effective secondary fermentation and will also ensure the kombucha is safe for consumption.

Typically for a gallon of strong kombucha, steeping 4 teabags in 4 cups of water and adding some sugar (1/4 to ½ cup) is sufficient to dilute it, but depending on the strength, a higher amount of freshly brewed tea may be used. Always cool the tea (and any other hot ingredients) to room temperature before mixing it with kombucha because excessive heat will kill the probiotics.

Because you will need to save starter liquid (for every one inch of SCOBY, I typically save one to two inches of starter liquid) and also to leave some room at the top of the jar so that the liquid doesn't spill over when the jar is moved, you will not get a true gallon when brewing 1 gallon of kombucha. The liquid yield is closer to ¾ gallon or less depending on how thick your SCOBY is. Similarly, when brewing kombucha in a 2-gallon jug, you will not get a full 2 gallons of kombucha. Most individuals brew either 1 gallon or 2 gallons of kombucha at a time, so I chose to focus my kombucha recipes on the 1-gallon batches. This means each recipe in this section calls for ¾ gallon of kombucha, but you can easily double the recipes if desired.

Don't Be Surprised If . . .

Don't be surprised when small SCOBYs form in the bottles during secondary fermentation. Because the probiotics and yeast continue to ferment, they form a colony during secondary fermentation, which is clear, gooey, and typically the size of a quarter. If you drink one by accident, nothing bad will happen, although the slimy texture going down your throat is not desirable for most people. Prior to drinking kombucha, use a fine strainer to catch whatever bacteria and yeast colonies (and/or fruit pulp that was added for flavor) have formed so that you can enjoy a SCOBY-free beverage.

Don't be surprised when your SCOBY forms long brown strings underneath it. These are colonies of yeast and they look kind of like kelp. They are completely normal and do not need to be cleaned out or removed. Some people mistakenly think these furry-looking strings are evidence that the SCOBY has gone bad, when they're actually evidence of a healthy SCOBY.

A Note About Safety

Making homemade kombucha can be risky if you are not careful. If you are new to making kombucha, please seek multiple sources to educate yourself about the process of brewing. It is very important to keep all instruments used in the process of making kombucha clean and to keep the SCOBY healthy. It is also important to avoid using ceramic or plastic for storing kombucha.

Use common sense and know that there is risk associated with fermentation. If you see a single spot of mold, abandon ship—throw out your whole SCOBY, discard all kombucha liquid, and completely sanitize the jar or jug you used to brew. Mold on kombucha looks similar to bread mold—it's usually circular, white or green, and fuzzy. I have made countless batches of kombucha and allowed my SCOBYs to sit in their starter liquid for a month at a time and I've never encountered mold. Have faith that as long as you follow the instructions and keep your SCOBY in a healthy environment, it will be safe.

Women who are nursing or pregnant should consult with their doctors before drinking kombucha. Because of the acidic and slightly alcoholic nature of kombucha, children younger than the age of six should not drink it. Children older than the age of six may drink kombucha in small volumes.

Please read instructions very carefully before starting a batch of kombucha. If you purchased your SCOBY online, the supplier likely included a list of instructions in the package. Chances are you can trust those instructions, but to double-check, be sure to read my instructions, too.

Kombucha should never smell or taste foul. It should taste slightly sweet yet vinegary and should smell this way, too. Home-brewed kombucha tends to be much stronger than store-bought kombucha, so the scent and taste will be much more pungent than store-bought kombucha. This is normal. If there is ever a putrid smell or the flavor does not sit right in your mouth, throw out the whole batch and start fresh with a new SCOBY.

Homemade kombucha can get so strong that drinking it is very similar to drinking vinegar. The optimal pH of kombucha should be on the acidic end, between 2.5 and 4.5. An acidic pH prohibits kombucha from becoming contaminated with bad bacteria. A pH lower than 2.5 is too acidic for human consumption and will need to be diluted before drinking. If the pH of your kombucha is ever below 2.5, add more tea and sugar and check the PH again before bottling it. A pH higher than 4.5 will create an environment that is optimal for bad bacteria to grow.

While it is perfectly fine to drink kombucha every day, most people caution against drinking more than 6 to 8 ounces of home-brewed kombucha each day. Commercially made kombucha is subject to many controls and tests, which makes it safe for drinking a larger amount. Since most people who brew kombucha (including myself) do not own advanced pH- and bacteria-testing equipment, it is wise to drink a lesser amount rather than risk upsetting the balance in your digestive system.

If you are concerned about sustaining a certain pH level in your kombucha, you can buy pH test strips to get a general idea of the how strong the kombucha is. For a more exact pH reading, you would need to buy a pH tester, as the pH test strips can give ambiguous readings. It is not necessary to test the pH of every kombucha batch, but I do recommend testing it periodically, especially when you think your kombucha is becoming too strong.

Should you brew a batch of bad kombucha and experience negative side effects, consult a doctor immediately. When in doubt, always, ALWAYS throw it out and start over. Provided the SCOBY you use to start your first batch of kombucha is healthy and provided you follow the instructions, it is unlikely a bad batch will result. Still, bad kombucha can cause harmful side effects, so play it safe.

Have fun with your home-brewed kombucha!

The active probiotics and yeasts in kombucha feed off of tea and sugar.

Basic Kombucha:

Ingredients (yields just under 1 gallon of kombucha):

- 1 kombucha SCOBY
- 1 (scant) gallon spring water or well water. Don't use water from your faucet because it probably has chlorine and/or fluoride in it.
- 10 black tea or green tea (no frills) tea bags*
- 1 cup cane sugar

**Be sure to use tea that is either 100 percent black or 100 percent green. Many companies add orange peel to black tea, which has essential oils in it that are not good for brewing. Stick to the 100 percent pure teas for the best results.*

You Will Also Need:

- Large pot for boiling water
- Large (1 gallon or more) glass jug/container for fermenting the kombucha
- Long-handled spoon for stirring
- Stick-on or floating thermometer
- Cheesecloth or breathable dish towel
- Stretchy rubber band
- A glass pitcher or other efficient method of transferring the kombucha from the jug to bottles or the dispenser you will be using to drink the kombucha out of
- Small fine strainer (we use a metal coffee strainer)
- Glass bottles with sealable lids. Both screw-top and flip-cap bottles work, and dark glass works best because kombucha does not like sunlight.

Optional Tools:

- Distilled white vinegar for cleaning your kombucha jug
- Heating device such as an electric heating pad. These work great for helping to maintain the temperature of your kombucha if your house is cold during the winter.
- Space blanket. May be used to trap in heat. During cold spells, wrapping the kombucha jug with a heating pad and securing it with a space blanket works wonders.

1. Add water to a sanitized pot before boiling

8 and 9. Covering your jug with cheesecloth allows the kombucha to breathe as it brews.

How to make homemade kombucha:

1. Sanitize everything you are using to make kombucha. You can do this by running it through the dishwasher, hand-washing in very hot water with soap, or by coating it in distilled white vinegar.

2. Boil water. If you are making 1 gallon of kombucha, you do not need to boil the entire 1 gallon—just enough (½ gallon or so) to brew the tea. This way you can add the remaining water to cool the tea once it's brewed.

3. Once water has reached a boiling point, remove it from heat and add tea bags. Steep the tea for 8 to 10 minutes and then remove the bags.

4. Add the cane sugar and stir well to dissolve.

5. Allow the tea to cool to roughly 75° to 85° (or if you only boiled half a gallon of water, add the remaining half gallon of cool water so that the hot water cools faster).

6. Once the tea is in the optimal temperature range, add the SCOBY (if this is your first time making kombucha and you bought your SCOBY online, simply remove it from its package and slip it in).

7. If you have a sticky thermometer that can be stuck to a surface, stick it on the outside of the jug (optional).

8. Cover the jug with cheesecloth so that the kombucha can continually breathe.

9. Secure the cheesecloth with a stretchy rubber band.

10. Place jug in a dark place (closet) that stays relatively warm and is not disturbed by people and light.

11. Allow kombucha to brew for five to seven days (the longer it brews, the more sugar it eats and the stronger it is).

12. Continually check the temperature of the kombucha. For best results, it should stay in the 70° to 85° range. If it falls below 70°, it's not a huge deal, it will just take longer for the kombucha to brew. If the kombucha gets above 85°, the probiotics may die. If you see any mold (it will look like bread mold . . . green/white and fuzzy circles), discard the SCOBY and the whole batch of kombucha.

13. When your kombucha is ready, remove the cheesecloth. NOTE: You will notice your SCOBY is bigger—it will grow to the width of the container it's in and a second SCOBY will form. SCOBYs will always continue to grow. Once a SCOBY gets to be a couple of inches thick, I recommend peeling a layer or two off and either discard it or give it to a friend along with some starter liquid so that they can brew their own kombucha.

14. Now that your kombucha has completed the first fermentation, you can either bottle it and be finished or add ingredients by following the recipes in this book. I find it is easiest to pour the kombucha liquid out of the jug and into a smaller pitcher. Using the pitcher, it is easy to pour the kombucha into bottles.

15. Once you have bottled the kombucha, you can either take a break, leave your SCOBY and starter liquid in the jug covered with cheesecloth bound with a rubber band, or you can brew a new batch. As long as SCOBYs are in a healthy environment, they can sit for months at a time between batches. When taking a break, simply leave the jug in a warm, dark place that doesn't get disturbed often (just as you would if you were brewing a batch) and be sure to inspect the SCOBY before brewing a new batch, especially if it has been sitting for more than a couple weeks. For every one inch of SCOBY, I typically save about two inches worth of starter liquid.

16. If you choose to add ingredients for a secondary fermentation, follow the recipe instructions and leave the bottles of flavored komucha at room temperature in a dark place for two to three days. During this process, the bacteria and yeast cultures eat the sugar you added (fructose from the juice or cane sugar) and continue to ferment. This makes the kombucha a little stronger and fizzy ("effervescent" is what the industry calls it). It is important to note that a small SCOBY will form in each bottle during the secondary fermentation, which can be strained out before drinking.

17. Place kombucha in the refrigerator for twenty-four hours before consuming for the best results. The cooler temperature will slow the fermentation (although the kombucha will continue to ferment), and refrigerating it seems to help in achieving a bubbly drink.

18. Get creative with your flavors, pat yourself on the back, and enjoy your homebrewed kombucha!

Pomegranate Kombucha (Kombucha and Juice)

I flavored the first few batches of kombucha I brewed using various 100 percent fruit juices, such as pomegranate, pear, blueberry, and cranberry. This is a very quick and easy way to add flavor as well as vitamins, minerals, and antioxidants to the kombucha.

Generally, 1 cup of juice per 1 gallon (or ¾ gallon) of kombucha is sufficient to put the kombucha through secondary fermentation. Pomegranate juice adds sweet, tart flavor as well as antioxidants.

Ingredients (yields just under 1 gallon of kombucha):

- 1 cup 100% pomegranate juice (or juice of choice)
- ¾ gallon kombucha (page 47)

Instructions

1. In a large pitcher or jug, combine the juice and the kombucha and stir well.
2. Pour the pomegranate kombucha into sealable bottles and leave them in a warm, dark place for two to three days for secondary fermentation.
3. Refrigerate the kombucha to slow the secondary fermentation.

Note:
When adding juice to kombucha for a secondary fermentation, the result does not come out as fizzy as if you added fresh fruit including the fruit pulp. Kombucha reacts more strongly during secondary fermentation when ingredients that have texture are added, resulting in a much fizzier beverage. Nevertheless, adding juice is tasty, healthful, and easy!

Lemon Ginger Kombucha

Lemon ginger kombucha is very handy to have on hand during cold and flu season! Not only does kombucha help boost the immune system, but both lemon and ginger are also great for fighting colds. Plus the beverage tastes great! When combined, lemon and ginger yields an almost creamy flavor, soothing the bite you'd expect from the ingredients on their own and leaving your palate happy!

Ingredients:

- 4 cups water
- 3 tablespoons fresh ginger, grated
- 3 tablespoons fresh lemon juice
- ½ cup cane sugar
- ¾ gallon kombucha (page 47)

Instructions:

1. Add the water and grated ginger to a pot and bring to a full boil. Reduce the temperature to medium and keep the water bubbling for about 5 minutes to infuse the water with ginger flavor.

2. Remove pot from heat and add the lemon juice and sugar, stirring to dissolve the sugar.

3. Allow the pot to sit until it cools to room temperature. This will allow the ginger to infuse the tea with flavor.

4. Once ginger tea is cool, add it to a pitcher or jug and combine it with the kombucha (depending on the size of your pitcher, you may need to do this in halves).

5. Stir kombucha and ginger tea together and then pour it into glass bottles. Try to get as much of the ginger in the bottles with the kombucha as possible. Secure with a tight cap.

6. Leave bottles in a warm, dark place for two to four days to allow it to undergo secondary fermentation. Refrigerate kombucha once the second ferment is complete to slow the fermentation.

7. When you're ready to drink the kombucha, strain it into a glass using a fine strainer to get the ginger pulp and newly grown SCOBY out. Discard the pulp and enjoy your healthy beverage!

Apple Cinnamon Kombucha

Apple cinnamon is my favorite kombucha flavor during the fall and winter months. The warm spices and sweet, tart apple make for a cozy beverage. Because the ingredients in this beverage are uncomplicated and easy to find any time of year at any grocery store, this is a great recipe to make in a large batch to store in bottles and enjoy for weeks.

Ingredients:

- 4 apple-flavored tea bags
- 4 cups water
- 1 teaspoon ground cinnamon
- ⅛ teaspoon ground nutmeg
- ½ cup sugar
- 3 ounces dried apple rings (no preservatives)*
- ¾ gallon kombucha (page 47)

**Purchase your dried apples from a natural food store to get them without preservatives. The ingredients list should be simple for any dried fruit you add to kombucha and it is worth paying a little extra to be sure the kombucha stays healthy and doesn't have an adverse reaction with unnecessary chemicals or ingredients.*

Instructions:

1. In a saucepan, add 4 cups of water and bring it to a boil.
2. Remove water from heat, add the apple-flavored tea bags, and steep tea for 5 to 8 minutes.
3. Add the sugar and stir to dissolve.
4. Set the sweetened apple tea aside and allow it to cool to room temperature. You can speed up this process by putting it in the refrigerator or an ice bath until it reaches a lukewarm temperature.
5. Slice apple rings in half and put two slices (one ring) in each bottle before filling it with kombucha. Seal the bottles.
6. Leave bottles in a warm, dark place for two to four days to allow kombucha to go through secondary fermentation.
7. Refrigerate the kombucha. When ready to drink, use a strainer to strain out the small SCOBY that formed in the bottle during secondary fermentation.

Blackberry Sage Kombucha

The tart and sweet blackberries give a great deal of life to the kombucha, as berries tend to make for a bubblier beverage and infuse very noticeable flavor. The sage gives the beverage a soft earthiness. Blackberries are rich in antioxidants and fiber. They aid in digestion, promote cardiovascular health, protect against cancer cells and neurological diseases, and more. Sage is an herb related to mint and is full of health benefits and medicinal uses. It is an anti-inflammatory, improves memory, can be used as an antiseptic, helps with allergic reactions and mosquito bites, and is packed with antioxidants!

Ingredients:

2 cups ripe blackberries

.65 ounces sage leaves, chopped (about 15 to 20 large sage leaves)

⅓ cup cane sugar

¾ gallon kombucha (page 47)

Instructions:

1. Heat blackberries in a saucepan, covered, over medium heat. As the blackberries heat up and begin to bubble and soften, mash them with a fork.

2. Once a pulpy juice forms add the sugar and sage and bring to a gentle boil.

3. Reduce heat to medium-low, cover the saucepan, and allow the flavors to cook together, about 15 to 20 minutes. Do not allow mixture to boil or cook for too long, or else it will become very thick.

4. In a large pot or pitcher, combine the kombucha and blackberry sage mixture. Mix together well and then pour the blackberry sage kombucha into sealable bottles, including the sage leaves and blackberry pulp. Seal the bottles.

5. Allow the kombucha to go through its secondary fermentation by allowing it to sit in a warm, dark place for two to three days. Note that the longer the kombucha sits, the more sugar will be eaten by the probiotics, which will result in a less sweet and more fizzy beverage.

6. Refrigerate for twenty-four hours after the secondary fermentation is complete. This slows the secondary fermentation, but the kombucha will continue to ferment and get fizzier the longer it sits in the refrigerator.

7. When you're ready to drink the kombucha, use a small fine strainer to strain out the sage leaves, blackberry pulp, and whatever small SCOBY has formed during the secondary fermentation. Discard all the pulp and enjoy the beverage!

Jasmine Kombucha

Although kombucha prefers 100 percent black tea for brewing, you can add other flavored teas can be added for secondary fermentation. Consider using your favorite tea flavors and even use loose tea.

This relaxing beverage smells and tastes wonderful. Jasmine makes a naturally soothing tea that is known for calming the mood and lowering heart rate. Studies show jasmine can prevent stroke and esophageal cancer. Jasmine tea adds a soft, floral flavor and is an easy way of flavoring kombucha for secondary fermentation.

Ingredients:

- 3 cups water
- 3 jasmine tea bags
- ½ cup sugar
- ¾ gallon kombucha (page 47)

Instructions:

1. In a saucepan, bring the water to a boil.
2. Add the tea bags and steep for 5 to 8 minutes.
3. Add the sugar and stir to dissolve.
4. Allow jasmine tea to cool to room temperature. To speed up this process, you can put the pot of tea in an ice bath or pour the tea in a jug and put it in the refrigerator until it reaches a lukewarm temperature.
5. In a large pitcher or jug, combine the jasmine tea with the kombucha and stir.
6. Pour jasmine kombucha into sealable bottles and then seal them shut.
7. Leave them in a warm, dark place for two to four days to allow for secondary fermentation.
8. Refrigerate the bottles after secondary fermentation. When ready to drink, open bottles carefully in case pressure built during secondary fermentation.

Pineapple Kombucha

Are you looking for that kombucha that is ultra fizzy and sweet? Well here it is! When pineapple chunks are added to kombucha for secondary fermentation, a very fizzy beverage results. I have found that the more acidic fruits yield the more effervescent probiotic beverages. For this reason, acidic fruits are great for flavoring these beverages, but it is important to use non-breakable bottles and to be very careful when opening the bottles after secondary fermentation.

Screw-top bottles are recommended for bottling this particular recipe, as the pressure that builds during secondary fermentation from the pineapple becomes so great that the beverage overflows when it is opened out of a flip-cap bottle. With screw tops, a minimal amount of air is always allowed out and you are able to slowly twist the cap to relieve pressure before opening. For safety purposes, do not hand children bottles of pineapple kombucha, as they may explode all over and can be unsafe for them to open. It is best to always look away from the bottle while carefully opening it and never point it at anyone. The same is true for any fizzy probiotic beverage in this book.

While pineapple kombucha requires a little additional forethought and precaution, it has an incredible tropical flavor and is so refreshing in the spring and early summertime when pineapples are in season!

Ingredients:

- 2 cups fresh pineapple, chopped into ¼" to ½" pieces
- ¾ gallon of homemade kombucha (page 47)

Instructions:

1. Evenly distribute the chopped pineapple between the bottles you're using for bottling.
2. Pour the kombucha into the bottles with the pineapple.
3. Seal the bottles and place them in a dark, warm spot, such as a cabinet or closet.
4. Allow bottles to sit for two to three days in a warm, dark place so that the kombucha goes through a secondary fermentation.
5. Refrigerate the kombucha for at least twenty-four hours before consuming. Allowing the kombucha to refrigerate for longer than a day will result in more effervescent kombucha.

Raspberry Mint Kombucha

The combination of raspberries and mint make a sweet, slightly tart, and refreshing beverage with an abundance of flavor. Fresh raspberries are heated with mint leaves to allow all the flavors to open up and infuse. Raspberry mint kombucha is a fun beverage any time of year, and is particularly great in the summer when raspberries are in season.

Ingredients:

- 6 ounces fresh raspberries
- .75 ounces fresh mint leaves, roughly chopped
- ½ cup sugar
- ¼ cup water
- ¾ gallon kombucha (page 47)

Instructions:

1. Remove mint leaves from the stems and using your fingers, rip them into smaller pieces (in half or thirds is fine).

2. Place raspberries, mint leaves, sugar, and water into a small saucepan and heat over medium. Bring mixture to a full boil.

3. Using a fork, smash the raspberries until they lose form.

4. Reduce heat to medium-low and allow the mixture to continue to boil gently for about 5 minutes to allow the mint to infuse.

5. Remove from heat and allow mixture to cool to room temperature. To speed up this process, pour it into a bowl or glass and place in the refrigerator.

6. In a large pitcher or jug, combine the kombucha and raspberry-mint mixture.

7. Stir to combine, then pour the kombucha into bottles.

8. Once you reach the bottom, spoon the raspberry and mint pulp into the bottles, trying to distribute the pulp evenly among the bottles.

9. Leave the bottles in a dark, warm place for two to four days to allow the kombucha to go through secondary fermentation.

10. Refrigerate at least twenty-four hours before drinking. The kombucha will get fizzier the longer you wait to drink it.

11. When you're ready to drink the kombucha, use a fine strainer to strain out the newly formed SCOBY and the raspberry and mint pulp. Enjoy!

Fig Kombucha

Incorporating figs into kombucha, smoothies, or even baked goods is an excellent way of achieving a naturally sweet treat. Figs are high in fructose and have a subtle flavor, making them a wonderful way to add sweetness without overpowering flavor. This is a fizzy and sweet kombucha with nothing but "original" flavor. Using 1 fig per 16-ounce bottle, you can scale this recipe to any size you would like. If you use the full ¾ gallon, you will end up with 6 bottles.

Ingredients (yields just under 1 gallon of kombucha):

- 6 ripe figs, chopped into small bits
- ¾ gallon kombucha (page 47)

Instructions:

1. Add 1 finely chopped fig to each 16-ounce bottle.
2. Seal bottles and leave them in a warm dark place for two days for secondary fermentation.
3. Refrigerate fig kombucha for a full twenty-four hours for best result before consuming.
4. When ready to consume, strain the fig pulp (and the newly-formed SCOBY) using a fine strainer and enjoy!

Jun

About Jun

Jun is a relative of kombucha and is brewed the exact same way kombucha is, except it is fermented using honey and green tea as opposed to sugar and black tea. Jun is brewed using a Symbiotic Culture of Bacteria and Yeast (SCOBY). It is important to note that a jun SCOBY is different from a kombucha SCOBY. For this reason, jun cannot be brewed using a kombucha SCOBY, just like one cannot brew kombucha using a jun SCOBY. The bacteria cultures are not interchangeable and both cultures prefer a specific type of food. When brewing jun, take the exact same precautions you would when brewing kombucha.

While the flavor of Jun is similar to the flavor of kombucha, the honey flavor in jun is prevalent and causes it to taste creamy, whereas kombucha tends to taste vinegary. For this reason, when flavoring jun, stronger flavors are necessary to mask the flavor of honey if that is your goal. In general, berries and strong spices and herbs work best for flavoring jun, as softer flavors tend to be over-powered by the honey. While there may be small-scale jun distributors, it is far less popular than kombucha and there is not yet a major commerical jun producer.

Health Benefits of Jun

Just like kombucha, jun helps create balance in the digestive system and can alleviate digestive problems and discomfort. Jun can also treat and prevent arthritis or other joint inflammation, boosts the immune system, and help increase energy.

Shelf Life

When sealed properly in bottles, jun will stay fresh in your refrigerator for up to one month. For this reason, it is never a bad idea to make large batches of jun to have on hand at any given time

Notes About Brewing Jun

Each time you brew a batch of jun, a new SCOBY will form. It is perfectly fine to allow the SCOBYs to continue to grow, but I have found the best results with SCOBYs that are no more than two to three inches thick. Just as you can with a kombucha SCOBY, you can peel off a layer and give it to friends or family so they can start their own batch.

Note that long, brown, seaweed-like strings will form underneath your SCOBY after you have brewed several batches. These are strains of yeast and are completely healthy and normal. There is no reason to clean them off or discard them.

Because you will need to save some of the starter liquid (I usually save two inches of starter liquid for every one inch of SCOBY) and the SCOBY takes up space, a 1-gallon batch of jun will not yield a useable full gallon—you will get more like ¾ of a gallon, which is why all of the recipes in this section call for ¾ gallon of jun.

Follow all safety precautions when brewing jun as you would when brewing kombucha, making sure to always brew using glass containers and be mindful of the temperature range of your home so that your SCOBY and jun stay healthy.

Prior to brewing a batch of jun, I recommend carefully reading the kombucha section, as all of the same rules apply.

Basic Jun

Ingredients:

- 1 jun SCOBY plus starter liquid
- 1 (scant) gallon spring or well water
- 8 to 10 green tea bags
- ½ to ¾ cup honey

Note:
The supplier of your jun SCOBY will likely include a page of instructions. Use the portion of water, sugar, and tea that your supplier recommends, especially if the SCOBY is small, as 1 gallon may be too much to start with, depending on the diameter and thickness of your SCOBY.

You Will Also Need:

- Large pot for boiling water
- Large (1 gallon or more) glass jug/container for fermenting the jun
- Long-handle spoon for stirring
- Stick-on or floating thermometer
- Cheesecloth or breathable dish towel
- Stretchy rubber band
- A glass pitcher or other efficient method of transferring the jun from the jug to bottles or the dispenser you will be using to drink the jun out of.
- Small fine strainer (we use a metal coffee strainer)
- Glass bottles with sealable lids. Both screw-top and flip-cap bottles work. Dark glass works best because jun does not like sunlight.

Instructions:

1. Heat half a gallon of water in a pot on the stove until it boils.
2. Remove the pot from heat and add the tea bags. After a couple of minutes, pour in the honey, stir, and allow the tea to continue to brew another 5 to 8 minutes.
3. Remove the teabags from the pot and discard them.
4. To bring the temperature of the water down, add the other half gallon of water to the pot of tea.

5. Using a thermometer, test the temperature of the tea. It needs to be between 75° and 85° Fahrenheit for proper brewing. Your goal is to keep the jun within this temperature range while it is brewing, although it will survive temperatures that are not too far outside of this range.

6. Once the tea is in the optimal temperature range, pour it into a large glass jug or jar. Add the jun SCOBY with the jun starter fluid (jun starter fluid is simply brewed jun).

7. Cover the jug with a cheesecloth or kitchen towel fastened with a rubber band. Place the jun in a dark and warm (between 75° and 85°) place for five to seven days. The longer the kombucha brews, the less residual sugar content it will have, and the stronger it will be. The jun is ready when it no longer tastes like tea sweetened with honey and has a desirable strength (to your taste).

8. Once the jun has finished fermenting, you have two options. You can either stop here, bottle and refrigerate it, or you can add more tea with honey, fruit, herbs, and/or flowers to flavor the jun and allow it to go through a secondary fermentation process. If you choose to flavor the jun, follow the recipes in this section (or try the recipes in the kombucha section, replacing any sugar with honey!).

9. Begin a new batch of jun by starting the whole process over, or cover the jun with a cheesecloth and store in a warm, dark place until you are ready to brew your next batch.

For more detailed information on the safety precautions and brewing process of jun, read the instructions in the Kombucha section (pages 37–45).

Blueberry Basil Jun

Mixing herbs with fruit to concoct flavors yields marvelous results! While one may think herbs are only for cooking savory meals, they are great companions to just about any fruit. The blueberry and basil combination is one of my all-time favorites. The cheery berry flavor in conjunction with the sweet, earthy basil makes for a completely unique, tasty, and fun drink. Get creative and adventurous with your fruit and herb combinations—it is pretty tough to go wrong here!

Ingredients:

- 1 pint fresh blueberries (2 cups)
- .75 ounces basil leaves, chopped
- 2 tablespoons honey
- ½ cup water
- ¾ gallon jun (page 69)

Instructions:

1. Add blueberries, basil leaves, water, and honey to a saucepan and heat covered until mixture reaches a full boil.
2. Reduce heat and allow mixture to gently boil for about 5 minutes to infuse flavors.
3. Remove saucepan from heat and allow it to cool to room temperature. To speed up this process, pour blueberry mixture into a bowl and refrigerate until cooled.
4. Combine the blueberry basil mixture with the jun in a pitcher. Pour mixture into sealable glass bottles and make sure they are sealed tight.
5. Leave the bottles at room temperature in a dark place for two days to allow for secondary fermentation.
6. Place bottles in the refrigerator for twenty-four hours before consuming for the best results.
7. Prior to drinking, strain the blueberry and basil pulp from the jun using a fine strainer.

Chai Jun

It is amazing how just a little spice can completely change the flavor of a beverage. For chai tea lovers, this is the perfect addition to your jun or kombucha. It is one of the easiest recipes and makes a wonderful beverage with the perfect sweet and spicy balance. You can either make your own chai spice at home using spices you probably already have on hand, or you can purchase chai spice from virtually any grocery store.

This is a great drink for any time of year and is particularly wonderful during the fall and winter when you crave warm spices like cinnamon and nutmeg. Having chai seasoning around during the fall and winter is wonderful for baking or even adding to your hot chocolate or coffee. If you want to take this drink a step further, you can scrape the insides of a couple of fresh vanilla beans to turn this into Vanilla Chai Jun!

Ingredients:

- 4 cups water
- 3 green tea bags
- ¼ cup honey
- 4 teaspoons chai spice (see recipe on previous page or use store-bought)
- ¾ gallon jun (page 69)
- 2 vanilla beans, insides scraped, optional

You can use leftover chai spice for flavoring other beverages in this book or for baking goodies!

Homemade Chai Spice:

- 2 teaspoons ground cinnamon
- 1 teaspoon ground cardamom
- 1 teaspoon ground ginger
- ½ teaspoon ground nutmeg
- ¼ teaspoon ground cloves
- Pinch black pepper

Instructions:

1. Heat 4 cups of water in a saucepan and bring to a boil.
2. Remove from heat and steep 3 green tea bags for 5 to 8 minutes.
3. If adding vanilla beans, carefully make a long incision down the length of the vanilla beans using a knife. Spread them open and scrape out the insides. Add the insides to the tea and stir.
4. Add the honey and the chai seasoning and stir to dissolve.
5. Allow mixture to cool to room temperature.
6. In a large jug, combine half a gallon of jun and the chai tea. Stir and then pour the Chai Jun into sealable bottles.
7. Leave the bottles in a dark place at room temperature for two to three days.
8. Refrigerate for twenty-four hours before drinking for best results.

Rose Jun

Roses are great for more than just Valentine's Day and anniversaries. Rose water is used quite frequently in baking and when the petals are steeped into a tea (often called "rose hip tea"), a wonderful aroma and calming flavor results. There are quite a few medicinal aspects to rose tea. It is full of antioxidants, is a natural laxative, cleanses the liver and gall bladder, can help relieve depression, and is full of vitamin C, D, K, and E. Get this: rose tea can also help provide regularity in your digestive tract and promote healthy gut flora—add this to the probiotics in jun and you've got yourself a digestive cure-all!

Ingredients:

- 5 cups spring or well water
- 1 cup dried rose buds
- ½ cup honey
- ¾ gallon jun (page 69)

Instructions:

1. Heat the water in a saucepan until boiling.
2. Add the dried rose buds and steep tea for 10 minutes.
3. Stir in the honey and allow the rose tea to cool all the way to room temperature (you can refrigerate it to speed up the process).
4. In a large pitcher or jug, combine the rose tea and jun, including the rose buds.
5. Pour the rose jun into sealable containers. Distribute the rose buds amongst the bottles. This will continue to infuse rose flavor into the jun as well as help with secondary fermentation.
6. Seal bottles well and leave them in a warm, dark room for two to three days.
7. Refrigerate for at least twenty-four hours before drinking for the best results.
8. When ready to drink, use a fine strainer to strain the rose buds and the SCOBY that formed during secondary fermentation. Enjoy!

Hibiscus Jun

Hibiscus jun is full of color, flavor, and health benefits! When brewed into tea, hibiscus has a sweet, tart, citrusy flavor which is refreshing and floral. Hibiscus tea is full of antioxidants, vitamin C, and is even great for your heart. It has been said that hibiscus tea can help people lose weight because it contains an amylase inhibitor, which inhibits sugars from releasing into the blood stream.

Ingredients:

- 6 cups water
- 2/3 cup hibiscus flowers
- ½ cup honey
- ¾ gallon jun (page 69)

Instructions:

1. In a small saucepan, heat the water until it boils.
2. Add the hibiscus flowers, remove saucepan from heat, and allow hibiscus tea to steep for 8 minutes with the pot covered.
3. Add the honey and stir to dissolve.
4. Allow the tea to cool until it's room temperature.
5. Once cool, add the tea (straining the hibiscus flowers out and discarding) and the jun to a large pitcher or jug and stir to combine.
6. Pour the hibiscus jun into well-sanitized sealable bottles.
7. Leave the bottles sealed at room temperature for two to three days.
8. Refrigerate at least twenty-four hours before drinking for best (effervescent) results.

Green Jun

Superfood or "green drink" powders can be purchased from any natural food store and most vitamin shops. They contain a large concentration of powdered vegetables and fruit to ensure you get a high density of nutrients in one scoop. Adding this powder to jun or kombucha infuses more health benefits and also helps to flavor the beverage. Not all green drinks are created equal, so use a powder that you have either used before or purchase one on someone's recommendation. If purchasing over the Internet, read reviews, as the quality of the powder will affect the outcome of the jun's secondary fermentation.

Because there is natural fructose in the powders, the probiotics in the jun feed off these sugars, which allows the drink to go through secondary fermentation and become slightly fizzy.

Ingredients:

- ¾ gallon jun (page 69)
- ½ cup superfood green drink powder

Instructions:

1. Pour the jun into a large pitcher and add the green drink powder.
2. Stir vigorously until well incorporated.
3. Pour the green jun into sealable bottles and secure the lids.
4. Leave the bottles in a warm, dark place for two to three days.
5. Refrigerate the bottles to slow the secondary fermentation. Use a fine strainer to strain the SCOBY that formed during secondary fermentation prior to drinking.

Watermelon Lime Jun

During the summer time, agua fresca, which is a pureed fruit beverage, is refreshing and tasty. This jun recipe is simply puréed seedless watermelon with lime and honey to add a crisp, refreshing flavor. Because watermelons yield a high volume of fruit and they're easy to find in the summer, this is a great recipe to make in a large batch to have on hand during the heat of the year.

Ingredients:

- 5 cups seedless watermelon, chopped (about 3 cups worth when puréed)
- 2 limes, juiced
- 3 tablespoons honey
- ¾ gallon jun (page 69)

Instructions:

1. Add the chopped watermelon, lime juice, and honey to a blender and blend until completely smooth.
2. In a large pitcher, combine the watermelon purée with the jun and stir well to incorporate.
3. Pour the watermelon lime jun into sealable bottles and secure their lids.
4. Leave bottles in a warm, dark room for two to three days.
5. Refrigerate the bottles prior to drinking and use a fine strainer to remove any SCOBY that has formed during secondary fermentation.

Strawberry Jun

When it comes to jun and kombucha, strawberry is always a winning flavor, making this a beverage most people will enjoy. This is a great introduction-to-jun recipe, as it is easy to make and palatable for those who are unfamiliar with jun's flavor. Strawberries and honey make a soft, wonderful medley and great flavor combination.

Ingredients:

- 3 cups fresh ripe strawberries, chopped
- ¼ cup spring or well water
- ½ cup honey
- ¾ gallon jun (page 69)

Instructions:

1. Heat the strawberries and water in a saucepan until boiling.

2. Reduce heat and simmer, covered, for 10 to 20 minutes until strawberries have completely lost their form. You can mash them with a fork to create a uniform substance.

3. Remove from heat, stir in honey, and allow mixture to cool completely.

4. In a large pitcher or jug, combine the strawberry mixture and the jun and stir.

5. Pour the strawberry jun (including strawberry pulp—it will help with secondary fermentation) in sealable bottles, leaving a little space at the top of the bottle because pressure will build. Seal the bottles well.

6. Place bottles in a dark room or closet for two to three days to allow for secondary fermentation.

7. Refrigerate the strawberry jun for at twenty-four hours before drinking for optimal results. When ready to drink, strain the strawberry pulp using a fine strainer.

Apricot Jun

Apricots tend to be the forgotten stone fruit, but they are wonderful for flavoring any beverage in this book. They provide a soft, subtly sweet flavor. The apricot pulp helps to create a fizzy beverage during secondary fermentation and adds sweetness while maintaining much of the natural flavor of the jun.

Ingredients:

- 4 large ripe apricots, pitted and chopped
- ¼ cup water
- ¼ cup honey
- ¾ gallon jun (page 69)

Instructions:

1. Add chopped apricots and water to a medium saucepan. Cover and bring the mixture to a boil.

2. Reduce the heat and allow the mixture to continue to boil gently, covered, until the apricots lose their form, about 10 minutes.

3. Remove from heat and add honey.

4. Allow apricot mixture to cool completely.

5. In a large pitcher (or two pitchers), add the apricot mixture and the jun.

6. Stir well and pour into sealable bottles.

7. Leave at room temperature in a dark place for three days.

8. Refrigerate for twenty-four hours or more.

9. When ready to drink, use a strainer to strain the jun into a glass. There will be bits of apricot pulp and small colonies of bacteria and yeast that will have formed, so for best results, straining the jun before drinking is recommended.

Rhubarb Jun

Perhaps one of the most distinctive beverages in this book, rhubarb jun carries a wonderfully unique flavor and is fun to make. While rhubarb stalks can seem intimidating to those who have never cooked with them, rhubarb gives a sweet, tart, somewhat peppery taste and is a wonderful change-up from regular fruit flavors. Rhubarb is high in vitamins C and K, antioxidants, lutein, and calcium, making it an immunity-boosting plant.

Ingredients:

- 1 stalk rhubarb (about 1 cup chopped)
- 1 cup water
- $^{1}/_{3}$ cup honey
- $^{3}/_{4}$ gallon jun (page 69)

Instructions:

1. Add the chopped rhubarb and water to a saucepan. Cover and heat over medium.
2. Bring the mixture to a full boil, then reduce the heat and allow it to bubble gently (still covered) until the pieces of rhubarb are completely softened and lose form.
3. Add the honey and stir to dissolve.
4. Remove the mixture from heat and allow it to cool completely. To speed up this process, pour the mixture into a container and refrigerate it.
5. Combine the cooled rhubarb mixture and the jun in a large pitcher and stir well.
6. Pour the rhubarb jun into sealable glass bottles. Distribute the rhubarb pulp as evenly as possible among the bottles and secure the tops.
7. Leave the bottles in a warm, dark room for two to three days.
8. Refrigerate the jun for twenty-four hours to slow the secondary fermentation process.
9. When ready to drink, strain the jun using a fine strainer, discarding the jun pulp and the newly formed SCOBY.

Lacto-fermented Lemonade

About Lacto-fermented Lemonade

The term, *lacto-fermented* can be applied to all sorts of fermented foods and beverages, such as sauerkraut, pickles, or ginger beer. Lacto-fermented lemonade is a probiotic lemonade, fermented using water, fresh lemon juice, sugar, and whey. This drink gets its probiotic qualities from whey, which is the watery substance that forms on top of yogurt. When mixed with lemon juice and sugar water, the whey continues to culture and probiotics continue to multiply.

This refreshing beverage can be flavored to be a seasonal treat any time of year and it is particularly refreshing in the summertime. The whey gives the lemonade a creamy flavor, making it taste similar to lemon meringue pie, by far the most unique lemonade you will ever taste! This beverage is healthier than normal lemonade because the probiotics in the whey eat up some of the sugar, leaving the beverage sweet but with less sugar content than what it started with.

This is one of the easiest probiotic beverages to make and takes a relatively small time commitment. It is also cost effective and can be made in large batches for friends and family to enjoy.

Probiotic Lemonade and Secondary Fermentation . . . Or Not

Lacto-fermented lemonade is the only water-based probiotic beverage that I choose not to put through secondary fermentation. The effervescence and flavor profile does not seem to change when fermented a second time, so I skip secondary fermentation altogether. If you are curious about trying it, don't let me hold you back! You can still follow any of the recipes in this section and simply add the extra step of leaving bottled lacto-fermented lemonade at room temperature for a couple days to see if anything happens through secondary fermentation.

A Note About Sweeteners:

Lemonade seems to taste the best when it is sweetened using fruit and cane sugar. For those who try to avoid cane sugar, it can be replaced using agave or maple syrup to taste. Some of the cane sugar used to ferment the beverage is metabolized in the process, which leaves it tasting sweet even though the glycemic level decreases. Just about any fruit or herb goes wonderfully in lacto-fermented lemonade, so don't be shy about experimenting with flavors!

Kerr

Lacto-fermented Lemonade

Ingredients:

- ¾ cup sugar
- 1 gallon water
- 1½ cups fresh lemon juice (about 10 to 14 lemons)
- 1 cup whey (strained from 1 quart of whole milk yogurt)*

**You can get whey from low fat or non-fat yogurt, but it seems to be easiest to obtain it from whole milk yogurt.*

Instructions:

1. The easiest method to obtain whey is to strain it off yogurt. To do this, fold cheesecloth over onto itself and lay it over a bowl. Pour 32 ounces (1 quart) of whole milk yogurt (either store-bought or homemade) onto the cheesecloth. Take all of the edges of the cheesecloth and bring them together so that you have a bundle of yogurt. Use a rubber band to secure the cheesecloth around the yogurt completely.
Once you have your bundle secured, use one or two additional rubber bands to hang it from a cabinet or shelf over the mixing bowl so that the gravity helps drain the whey from the yogurt. It should only take about 20 to 30 minutes to strain a full cup of whey off the yogurt but if you don't have a full cup by this time, wait longer. Once your whey is strained, you will be using it for the lacto-fermented lemonade. Plus, guess what? You now have Greek yogurt in that cheesecloth! Simply pour/scrape the strained yogurt off the cheesecloth into a sealable container and enjoy it later! In a sealable gallon jar or jug, combine the whey, lemon juice, and sugar. Add the water and stir very well to dissolve the sugar. Note that the probiotics in the whey feed off of the sugar, so you will need to adjust the amount of sugar to your personal taste. If you desire a sweeter beverage, use up to 1 cup of sugar instead of ¾ cup.

2. Seal the container and allow it to sit at room temperature for two days. A closet, shelf, or pantry works great for storage.

3. Once the lacto-fermented lemonade is ready, you can refrigerate it and drink it cold, or add ingredients to it to flavor it, given by my recipes in this section.

4. To store the lemonade, simply bottle it in sealable bottles and keep it in the refrigerator for up to two weeks.

Raspberry Lemonade

If you are anything like me, you went crazy over raspberry lemonade as a kid when your family went out to dinner. Maybe you still do! Because we never made lemonade at home growing up, I loved getting refill after refill of sugary raspberry lemonade as a special treat to go alongside my cheeseburger and fries. While I no longer drink the high glycemic, artificial color- and flavor-ridden drink I used to covet, I now make it at home, and the flavor is worlds better!

Not only is this beverage much more natural than any store-bought lemonade, but it is also filled with probiotics. The raspberries kick in antioxidants for good measure, making this a healthful, yet kid-friendly, drink.

Ingredients:

- 2 pints fresh raspberries
- Juice of 2 meyer lemons
- ½ cup water
- 3 tablespoons sugar or agave nectar
- 8 cups lacto-fermented lemonade (page 91)

Instructions:

1. Add raspberries, lemon juice, and water to a saucepan. Cover and bring it to a gentle boil.

2. Reduce the heat but allow mixture to continue to bubble gently until the raspberries lose their form and juices are seeping out, about 5 to 8 minutes. Use a fork to smash the raspberries.

3. Add the sugar and stir, allowing it to dissolve.

4. Remove saucepan from the heat and allow it to cool completely.

5. Using a fine metal strainer, strain the mixture into a pitcher, jug, or large bottle to get all of the raspberry seeds out. Press on the raspberry pulp to ensure you get as much liquid out of the pulp as possible.

6. Discard the raspberry pulp.

7. Add the lacto-fermented lemonade to the pitcher and stir to combine.

8. Either serve the raspberry lemonade immediately or pour it into two bottles to save in the refrigerator (drink what won't fit into the bottles).

Sage Lacto-fermented Lemonade

Chances are, you have never had sage in a beverage, let alone lemonade. Before I lose your attention, hear me out. Sage is not only great in cooking savory foods, it also brings wonderful flavor to beverages. The subtle earthy flavor with the crisp, sweet lemonade is very drinkable and refreshing. While there are plenty of beverages in this book that are an "acquired taste," the herb-filled ones like this sage lemonade definitely are not, contrary to what one might think.

Sage contains Vitamin K and is a natural anti-inflammatory and antioxidant, and studies have shown regular intake of sage boosts memory.

Ingredients:

- 1 cup water
- 10 sage leaves, chopped
- Juice of 1 lemon
- 2 tablespoons sugar or agave nectar
- 4 cups lacto-fermented lemonade (page 91)

Instructions:

1. In a saucepan, bring the water and sage leave to a boil.
2. Remove from heat, add sugar, and stir to dissolve. Allow mixture to sit at room temperature at least 10 minutes to allow the sage flavor to infuse.
3. Pour the liquid into a container and refrigerate until cold.
4. Once the mixture has cooled all the way, strain the liquid into a pitcher, discarding the sage leaves.
5. Add the lacto-fermented lemonade to the pitcher and stir to combine.
6. Enjoy immediately or pour into sealable bottles and save for up to one week.

Strawberry Rhubarb Lemonade

As if strawberry lemonade weren't wonderful enough, strawberry rhubarb lemonade is even more delicious! The winning combination of strawberries and fresh rhubarb seems to be a crowd pleaser in any form, from baked goods to cocktails. Rhubarb is rich in calcium, antioxidants, lutein (which is great for your eyes), and Vitamin K. Stock up on rhubarb stalks for this tasty lemonade and also try Rhubarb Jun.

Ingredients:

- 1½ cups fresh rhubarb, chopped
- 1 cup water
- 1½ cups strawberries, chopped
- 1 lemon, juiced
- ¼ cup sugar
- 8 cups lacto-fermented lemonade (page 91)

Instructions:

1. Add water and rhubarb to a saucepan and bring to a boil, covered.
2. Reduce heat to a low boil and allow mixture to bubble and cook about 15 minutes.
3. Add strawberries, lemon juice, and sugar and cook an additional 3 minutes.
4. Allow mixture to cool before pouring it in a bowl or large glass and refrigerating until completely cold.
5. Add the strawberry rhubarb mixture and lacto-fermented lemonade to a blender.
6. Blend until smooth and serve chilled!

Lavender Lacto-fermented Lemonade

You're looking at the most relaxing lemonade you will ever drink! Lavender has been used in cultures worldwide for thousands of years for its laundry list of healing properties. Lavender buds contain polyphenols, which help fight bad bacteria and can ease bloating. In this sense, lavender and probiotics work miracles together for easing stomach pain and aiding digestion. Lavender also relieves dry and itchy skin and can also help heal open wounds. When steeped into a tea, lavender creates a soothing, floral, delicious elixir to calm the mind and body. Not to mention it makes one heck of a lemonade!

Ingredients:

- 1 cup water
- 1½ tablespoons lavender buds
- ¼ cup sugar
- Juice of 1 lemon
- 8 cups lacto-fermented lemonade (page 91)

Instructions:

1. In a saucepan, bring the water and lavender buds to a boil. Remove from heat and add the sugar and lemon juice, stirring to dissolve the sugar.
2. Allow mixture to sit for at least 20 minutes to allow the lavender flavor to infuse into the water.
3. Pour the mixture into a container and refrigerate until completely cold.
4. Using a strainer, strain the liquid into a pitcher, discarding the lavender buds.
5. Add the lacto-fermented lemonade and stir to combine.
6. Blend until smooth and serve chilled!

Blackberry Lemonade

I have fond memories of going blackberry picking with my family as a child. Where I grew up, blackberry bushes grew rampant and each blackberry season we would bring huge bowls with us to pick fresh, ripe blackberries straight from the vine. Sure, my small hands would get scraped by the thorns, but that was nothing compared to the enjoyment I got from eating freshly picked berries, saving some to be made into jams.

Blackberries are chock-full of antioxidants and have a very distinct and delicious flavor. This berry is great for flavoring any beverage in this book and transforms lacto-fermented lemonade into a fancy, tasty beverage that can be enjoyed by all!

Ingredients:

- 2 cups blackberries
- Juice of 2 lemons
- ½ cup water
- 3 tablespoons sugar
- 8 cups lacto-fermented lemonade (page 91)

Instructions:

1. Add blackberries, lemon juice, and water to a saucepan. Cover and bring it to a gentle boil.

2. Reduce the heat but allow mixture to continue to bubble gently until the blackberries lose their form and juices are seeping out, about 5 to 8 minutes. Use a fork to smash the blackberries.

3. Add the sugar and stir, allowing it to dissolve.

4. Remove saucepan from the heat and allow it to cool completely.

5. Using a fine metal strainer, strain the mixture into a pitcher, jug, or large bottle to get all of the blackberry seeds out. Press on the blackberry pulp to ensure you get as much liquid out of the pulp as possible.

6. Discard the blackberry pulp.

7. Add the lacto-fermented lemonade to the pitcher and stir to combine.

8. Either serve the blackberry lemonade immediately or pour it into two bottles to save in the refrigerator (drink what won't fit into the bottles).

Apricot Lemonade Slushy

Who says yogurt gets all the smoothie fun? Using other beverages in this book for fruit slushies or smoothies is brilliant and fun! Lacto-fermented lemonade is a particularly wonderful beverage to blend up with fruit and other ingredients because it is so well balanced with sweet and zesty flavor. Using this drink, particularly in the spring and summertime, in conjunction with in-season fruit, is sure to make a tasty and healthful beverage!

I find that lemonade and apricots go surprisingly well together, although I have not had much success making lemonade using apricots because of how thick and pulpy they are. To make apricot lemonade requires a great deal of apricots to harvest the juices, and I don't like the idea of all the apricot pulp going to waste. So here is a happy medium! Simply freezing fresh chopped apricots and blending them with lemonade, bananas, and almond milk makes a unique and delicious slushy!

Ingredients:

- 2 apricots, pitted, chopped and frozen
- 1 frozen banana
- ½ cup lacto-fermented lemonade (page 91)
- ½ cup vanilla almond milk

Instructions:

Put all ingredients in a blender and blend until smooth slushy forms.

Lemon Meringue Pie Drink

As I mentioned at the beginning of this section, lacto-fermented lemonade has a very lemon-meringue-pie-like taste to it because of the whey. It is sweet, creamy, and tart, with a soft mouth feel, giving it the essence of a dessert. These characteristics inspired me to make a smoothie using lacto-fermented lemonade to mimic lemon meringue pie! As simple (and silly) as this drink may be, it is one of our household favorites!

Ingredients:

- 2 frozen bananas
- 8 ounces lacto-fermented lemonade (page 91)
- Juice of half a lemon
- 2 tablespoons coconut milk

Instructions:

Add all ingredients to a blender and blend until smooth.

Probiotic Arnold Palmer

When I think of hot days, I think of iced tea and lemonade. And then I think of Arnold Palmers. This quintessential summer beverage is the simple combination of iced tea and lemonade and makes an incredibly refreshing drink. Simply brew a batch of your favorite tea (I recommend black tea), cool it off in the refrigerator, and then mix it up with your homemade lacto-fermented lemonade!

Ingredients:

- Black tea bags
- Sugar (optional)
- Lacto-fermented lemonade (page 91)

Instructions:

1. On a stovetop, bring desired amount of water to a boil. Remove pot from the heat and add black tea bags (about 1 teabag per one cup of water). Steep for 5 to 8 minutes. If you prefer your tea sweet, be sure to add desired sugar while the tea is still hot and stir to dissolve.
2. Allow tea to cool quite a bit before transferring it to a pitcher and refrigerating it until completely cold.
3. Fill a glass with ice cubes and fill it half-way with lacto-fermented lemonade. Fill the remaining half with your favorite iced tea.

Ginger Beer

About Ginger Beer

Ginger beer is a naturally fizzy beverage with a sweet and spicy bite. Grated ginger is fermented in sugar water and lemon juice, allowing the natural yeasts in ginger to feed off sugar and multiply, creating a probiotic beverage. While ginger beer is a sweet, spicy, delicious beverage all on its own, it is infamous for its role in cocktails, particularly the Dark & Stormy, a mixture of ginger beer and rum, garnished with a slice of lime.

While many people use the phrases "ginger beer" and "ginger ale" interchangeably, there is a difference between the two beverages. Ginger beer is fermented for up to two or three weeks using a "ginger bug," whereas ginger ale is more of a ginger-flavored soda. While there are ginger ale beverages made with real ginger, most ginger ales are simply carbonated water with ginger flavor and sugar. Ginger ale does not go through the same fermentation process that ginger beer does.

Health Benefits of Ginger Beer

Ginger has a great deal of health benefits and is commonly used to ease upset stomach, nausea, or diarrhea. This tasty plant is an anti-inflammatory, which can help with migraines, and studies show fresh ginger helps to prevent and fight several types of cancer cells including breast, colon, ovarian, prostate, and lung cancer. Ginger is also known for cleansing the body of toxic chemicals, easing menstrual cramps, and much more!

Ginger Beer and Secondary Fermentation

Once ginger beer is finished with its primary fermentation, you may add additional sugar and/or other ingredients to flavor it (using the recipes in this section) and allow it to go through a secondary fermentation.

Flavoring Ginger Beer

Ginger beer is perhaps the easiest drink in this book to flavor because just about any type of fruit and/or herb goes wonderfully with ginger. The fact that there is already a great deal of sweet and spicy flavor in ginger beer provides a wonderful canvas for incorporating other sweet, sour, tart, or creamy flavors. In this way, the added ingredients are typically what one tastes first when drinking the ginger beer, with the spicy ginger coming through at the finish. Getting creative with fruit and herb combinations is easy when it comes to ginger beer and you are virtually guaranteed to end up with a delicious probiotic drink!

Shelf Life of Ginger Beer

When properly sealed in bottles, plain ginger beer can last for up to one month in the refrigerator, but for best results, drink within two weeks of brewing. When ingredients such as fruit are added to ginger beer, consume within one week for best results. While ginger beer can last even longer than this, it is best to err on the safe side when it comes to probiotics.

Just like the other water-based recipes in this book, it is important to use either bottled spring water or well water. Do not use tap water because it likely has chlorine in it, which is not good for fermentation.

A Note About the Recipes in this Section

As is always the case with probiotic beverages, be cautious when opening a bottle after secondary fermentation as pressure builds and the drink will be fizzy. Never point a bottle at your face (or at any other person) while opening, and never hand a bottle to a child to open.

Ginger Beer

Making ginger beer is a three-step process. We start by making a ginger bug, then ferment it using water, sugar, and lemon juice, then bottle it and allow it to sit for secondary fermentation. While it is possible to acquire some ginger starter from a friend who is brewing his or her own ginger beer, it is more likely that you will need to create your own starter, which is straight-forward and easy—it just requires some time and attention to detail.

Ingredients for the ginger bug:

- 3 tablespoons fresh ginger, peeled and grated, divided
- 3 tablespoons raw organic sugar, divided
- 2 cups water

You Also Need:

1. 1-quart glass jar or jug
2. Cheesecloth
3. Stretchy rubber band
4. 1-gallon jug

How to make ginger starter/ginger bug:

1. To start your ginger bug, add 1 teaspoon of the peeled and grated ginger and 1 teaspoon of the sugar to a jar (a 1-quart jar works great).

2. Add two cups of spring water (non-chlorinated) to the jar and stir.

3. Cover the jar with a cheesecloth or towel bound with a rubber band.

4. Allow jar to sit in a dark place for twenty-four hours.

5. Once a day for one week, add 1 teaspoon of sugar and 1 teaspoon of grated fresh ginger to the jar and stir well. This ensures your ginger starter stays fed and grows, similar to sourdough starter. Stir a couple times per day. During this process, natural yeasts are released and create a white substance at the bottom of the jar. This is where the probiotics come from.

6. After about three to five days (perhaps longer if your house is very cold), the liquid will begin bubbling when you stir it. Once you can hear bubbles without touching the jar, your ginger bug is ready to be used. This will take seven to ten days in a warm house, but longer in a cool house. If after seven days, your ginger bug is still not bubbling, continue adding a teaspoon of sugar and ginger until it does.

7. Use the liquid from ginger starter to make ginger beer (instructions below). Continue adding water, ginger, and sugar to the starter as you continue to use it for batches of ginger beer. If you ever see mold floating on top of the starter liquid, discard the starter and make a new one.

Ingredients for the Ginger Beer:

- 1 cup ginger starter (see above)
- 1 (scant) gallon of spring (mineral) or well water
- 1¼ cups sugar (raw organic cane sugar recommended)
- ½ cup fresh lemon juice
- ⅓ cup fresh ginger, grated

How to make ginger starter/ginger bug:

1. Fill a gallon-sized jug most of the way with spring or well water (do not use water from the tap unless your house runs on a well).

2. Add the sugar, lemon juice, grated ginger, and the ginger starter. Stir very well.

3. Cover the jug with a cheesecloth or towel bound by a rubber band and put it in a dark place at room temperature for eight to ten days. Mine took eight days, even in a very warm (80°F +) house.

4. Taste-test the mixture periodically to see if you need to add more sugar. The natural probiotics will eat the sugar, so if the beverage ever loses all of its sweetness, add a little more sugar (no more than 2 tablespoons at a time), but be careful not to overload the probiotics, as they can die when given too much sugar.

5. Stir the mixture once or twice a day. You will notice a white substance forming around the ginger at the bottom of the jug. This is the natural yeasts coming out of the ginger—it's a good sign! There will also be large bubbles forming on the surface of the liquid. The ginger beer is ready when the substance becomes bubbly when stirred (similar to when you're making the ginger starter).

6. Once the ginger beer is ready, give it a taste test. If it doesn't taste sweet, add additional sugar and ginger because once you bottle the brew, it goes through secondary fermentation and the probiotics continue to need to eat sugar. (Note: the recipes in this section give advice on how much sugar to add prior to bottling).

7. At this point, your options are to either bottle the ginger beer as-is or flavor it prior to bottling it. If you choose to flavor it, try the recipes in this section for ingredient ideas. Pour the liquid (including the ginger pulp) into sealable bottles and set them in a dark room for two to four days. This process makes the ginger beer very fizzy. The warmer the room, the faster the beverage gets fizzy, so open a bottle every day or so to check the fizz and level of sweetness. Both the fizz and sweetness is up to your taste but be very careful not to allow the bottles to sit for too long because they most definitely will explode.

8. Place bottles in the refrigerator to calm the fermentation process. Note that the ginger beer will continue to ferment in the refrigerator, so try to consume the beverage within a few days after secondary fermentation is complete for best results. Leaving it in the refrigerator for longer than a week will result in a "drier," less sweet ginger beer.

9. You can now brew another batch of ginger beer using the ginger starter you have been feeding. Because your ginger starter is now more mature, it will take a little less time to brew your second batch.

TROUBLESHOOTING

If it seems like either your ginger starter or ginger beer is taking a long time to come to life (get bubbly), don't worry. This is likely the result of the temperature of your home. Like many probiotic beverages, ginger beer is one of those that seems to be doing nothing for quite some time and then, all of a sudden, it's working.

At the end of secondary fermentation, is your ginger beer too dry (not sweet and very fizzy)? This is because the yeast consumed all the sugar that was in the bottle, leaving very little sweetness for you. Some people prefer drier ginger beer, but if you prefer it to be on the sweet side, simply make sure you add additional sugar (either cane sugar, fruit, or juice) prior to bottling your next batch.

Did you pop open a bottle of ginger beer after three days of secondary fermentation and it wasn't fizzy and it still tasted sweet? If this is the case, your ginger beer still contains residual sugar that needs to be eaten by the probiotics. This is okay! Simply leave the remaining bottles (if any) at room temperature to continue secondary fermentation. Because there was plenty of sugar in the beverage prior to bottling, it will simply take an additional day or two for the probiotics to consume the sugar and for the beverage to become fizzy. To prevent flat ginger beer, be sure there are small bubbles that rise from the bottom to the top of the liquid prior to bottling it for secondary fermentation, as this is a sign of probiotic activity. Keep in mind that even if your ginger beer does not get fizzy, it is still full of probiotics and is great for you!

If at any point you find mold on the surface of your ginger beer while it is brewing, throw the whole batch out, even if it is only a tiny bit of mold. Ginger beer is easy to remake (especially since you already have your ginger starter ready to go), and it is not worth sacrificing quality and health even if it is frustrating to have a failed batch.

Blood Orange Ginger Beer

Blood oranges get their name from the dark red fruit beneath the rind. This red flesh is the result of anthocyanins, which are antioxidants (the same type as those in blueberries). The anthocyanins only cause the flesh to become red when the oranges are exposed to cold weather while they are growing or after harvest. These anthocyanins are not found in other citrus fruits. Blood oranges are full of vitamin C, vitamin A, and folic acid.

Blood oranges have a distinctly different flavor from regular navel oranges. They have a stronger flavor—both sweet and tart—than regular oranges, making them an aromatic and very flavorful ingredient for adding to probiotic drinks.

Ingredients:

- Juice of three ripe blood oranges
- 2 tablespoons sugar
- 4 cups ginger beer (page 111)

Instructions:

1. Combine the blood orange juice, sugar, and ginger beer in a pitcher. Stir vigorously to dissolve the sugar.
2. Pour into sealable bottles and secure the lids.
3. Leave bottles at room temperature for 2 days to allow for secondary fermentation.
4. Place in the refrigerator to slow the secondary fermentation process.

Raspberry Basil Ginger Beer

Raspberry basil ginger beer is heavenly! All of the flavors work wonders together, making this a cool and refreshing, yet spicy, beverage. If you have never had a beverage made with fresh herbs, don't be scared! This drink does not come out tasting savory like a fresh basil pasta dish; instead, the basil adds a rounded, somewhat earthy flavor, giving balance to the tart and spicy aspects of the beverage. Raspberries work well with most herbs, so try this recipe using sage, mint, or even some rosemary!

Ingredients:

- 2 cups fresh raspberries
- 10 to 15 fresh basil leaves, chopped
- ½ cup spring or well water
- 2 tablespoons sugar
- 8 cups ginger beer (page 111)

Instructions:

1. Heat the raspberries, basil, and water in a saucepan over medium heat and cover it.

2. Bring the mixture to a full boil, then reduce the heat and simmer, covered, for 3 to 5 minutes, or until the raspberries begin to lose their form. Mash the raspberries with a fork.

3. Allow mixture to cool to room temperature. To speed up this process, pour the mixture into a container and refrigerate it until cool.

4. In a large pitcher, combine the raspberry-basil mixture with the ginger beer and stir well.

5. Pour the Raspberry Basil Ginger Beer into sealable bottles (including the fruit and basil pulp). If there is any raspberry or basil pulp left at the bottom of the pitcher, spoon it into the bottles.

6. Secure the lids on the bottles and leave them at room temperature for two to three days to allow for secondary fermentation.

7. Place bottles in the refrigerator to slow the fermentation. For best results, wait at least twenty-four hours before drinking the beverage as it will continue to ferment and become fizzy.

8. When ready to drink, use a fine strainer to strain out the raspberry and basil pulp and discard the pulp. Enjoy your delicious beverage!

Coconut Basil Ginger Beer

Coconut milk, basil, and ginger go together seamlessly. The three generate a creamy, sweet, spicy flavor. The creamy coconut milk calms the spice and effervescence of the ginger beer and the basil adds a unique flair. Note that this recipe does not involve secondary fermentation. The ingredients are combined with once-fermented ginger beer to be served immediately as a delicious beverage. This drink goes wonderfully with virtually any ethnic food, particularly curry dishes.

Ingredients:

- 10 leaves fresh basil, roughly chopped
- 1 tablespoon agave nectar (optional)
- ¾ cup coconut milk (full fat from a can recommended)*
- 4½ cups ginger beer (page 111)

**If your house is chilly, the coconut fat and water may separate in your can of coconut milk. If this is the case, simply stir it together as best you can.*

Instructions:

1. Heat the coconut milk, agave, and chopped basil over medium heat just until it comes to a gentle boil.

2. Remove from heat and allow it to sit about 5 to 10 minutes to let the basil flavor infuse.

3. Pour the mixture into a glass or container and refrigerate to cool completely.

4. Once cool, strain the basil from the coconut milk using a strainer and discard the basil. Mix the coconut milk mixture with the ginger beer.

5. Pour the Basil Coconut Ginger Brew into glasses. Note that the coconut milk will rise to the top of the glass and become a little foamy. You can leave it as is or stir it in with a spoon.

6. Serve chilled and enjoy!

Grapefruit Rosemary Ginger Beer

Infusing herbs with fruit juice creates unique and fun flavors. In this case, the earthy rosemary tones down the citrus zing of the grapefruit juice, lending to a well-rounded, very refreshing beverage. This recipe makes a great base for an alcoholic beverage. Consider using it for a fun and different Paloma, adding tequila for a boozy cocktail.

Ingredients:

- 4 cups (roughly 1 liter) ginger beer (page 111)
- Juice of 2 grapefruits (1 cup fresh grapefruit juice)
- 2 to 3 tablespoons agave nectar, optional
- 2 tablespoons fresh rosemary sprigs

Instructions:

1. In a small saucepan, gently heat the grapefruit juice with the rosemary and agave nectar until it reaches just under boiling point.

2. Remove from heat and allow to cool slightly.

3. Pour the juice with the rosemary sprigs into a container and refrigerate until completely cool.

4. Combine the ginger beer with cooled grapefruit/rosemary juice, leaving the sprigs of rosemary in the juice. Leaving the rosemary in will infuse the ginger beer with more rosemary flavor.

5. Either enjoy beverage immediately or pour into sealable bottles to allow for secondary fermentation. Leave bottles at room temperature for two to four days, then place bottles in the refrigerator to slow down fermentation.

6. When ready to drink, strain out the rosemary sprigs using a strainer and enjoy!

Key Lime Ginger Beer

When key limes come into season, cocktail enthusiasts rejoice. These tiny limes pack a great deal of flavor, making a zesty beverage fun and different. Key limes are also wonderful for baking treats, but their true colors shine through in beverages and create a drink that goes down easily. While key limes take some time to juice, and the juice yield is very small compared to regular limes, the effort is well worth it.

Ingredients:

- 4 cups ginger beer (page 111)
- 12 key limes, juiced
- 2 tablespoons agave nectar or to taste

Instructions:

1. Combine all ingredients in a pitcher and stir well.
2. Either enjoy the beverage immediately or pour it into sealable bottles for secondary fermentation. Leave the bottles at room temperature for two to three days. Place bottles in the refrigerator to chill prior to drinking.

Strawberry Ginger Beer

Adding fresh strawberries to homemade ginger beer yields a sweet, crisp, summery beverage. This recipe is straight-forward and takes very little time to prepare, making it a wonderful recipe to double or triple for keeping in bulk. While strawberry ginger beer is fabulous to drink on its own, it happens to make an incredible ginger beer float! Take a gander at the Strawberry Vanilla Ginger Beer Float recipe because probiotics can even make great desserts!

Ingredients:

- 2 cups fresh ripe strawberries, chopped
- ½ cup water
- 2 tablespoons sugar
- 8 cups ginger beer (page 111)

Instructions:

1. In a saucepan, heat the strawberries and water, covered, over medium heat. Allow the mixture to come to a boil.
2. Once the strawberries begin to lose their form, mash them with a fork. Stir in the sugar. The mixture will have the consistency of chunky syrup.
3. Allow the mixture to cool to room temperature. To speed up this process, pour it in a bowl and refrigerate until cooled.
4. Combine the strawberry mixture with the ginger beer in a pitcher or jug and stir well.
5. Pour the strawberry ginger beer into sealable containers (bottles with screw tops recommended).
6. Leave at room temperature for two days and then place bottles in the refrigerator.
7. When ready to dink, very carefully open the bottles, as pressure will have built.
8. Strain the strawberry chunks out of the ginger beer using a fine strainer and discard the chunks.
9. Enjoy your delicious strawberry ginger beer!

Strawberry Vanilla Ginger Beer Float

No section on ginger beer would be complete without a ginger beer float! If you have never tried a float using ginger beer, I highly recommend it! The first time I had a ginger beer float was at a sushi restaurant in Idaho. The float included green tea ice cream (always one of my favorites) and a particularly gingery ginger beer. I was intrigued by the flavor combination and was very pleased with the treat!

This Strawberry Vanilla float includes the health benefits of the probiotic ginger beer which, according to my calculations, means some of the guilt is taken out of the indulgent dessert. It is rich and creamy with a nice ginger spice to counterbalance the sweetness. There is a world of opportunity when it comes to flavor combinations for ginger beer floats, so feel free to get creative!

Ingredients:

- 1 pint vanilla bean ice cream
- 16 ounces homemade Strawberry Ginger Beer (page 125)

Instructions:

1. Load up tall glasses with desired amount of ice cream.
2. Carefully open a bottle of Strawberry Ginger Beer and using a strainer to strain out the strawberry pulp, pour the ginger beer over the ice cream.
3. Enjoy with friends!

Serves 3 to 4 people.

Other Ginger Beer Float Flavor Combinations:

Green tea ice cream and regular ginger beer
Mango sorbet and Pineapple Ginger Beer

Pineapple Ginger Beer

Don't let the simplicity of this recipe fool you, as this drink is packed with flavor and health benefits! Pineapple juice is known for settling indigestion, and the fact that ginger also helps ease nausea and upset stomach makes this the perfect drink for those experiencing digestive discomfort.

Pineapple juice is full of vitamin C, B6, and thiamine. It is also rich in an enzyme called bromelain, which aids digestion and helps break down the proteins in food. All factors considered, this beverage is very soothing on the stomach, boosts the immune system, and helps the gut with its important digestive function.

Ingredients:

- 2 cups 100% pineapple juice
- 7 cups ginger beer (page 111)

Instructions:

1. Combine the pineapple juice and ginger beer in a large pitcher.
2. Pour into sealable bottles and secure the lids.
3. Let bottles sit for two to three days in a warm, dark place.
4. Refrigerate for twenty-four hours before consuming for best results.

Water Kefir and Kefir Soda

About Water Kefir

Water kefir, not to be confused with milk-based kefir, is fermented using water kefir "grains." Just like milk kefir grains, water kefir grains are not real grains. They are colonies of yeast and bacteria that are somewhat translucent and shaped like miniature cauliflower florets. Water kefir grains require only water and sugar to ferment. While activating dehydrated kefir grains (explained in instructions below) can take two to three weeks, once the grains are active, the fermentation process goes relatively quickly. This dairy-free beverage is an outstanding method for taking in probiotics, staying hydrated, and detoxifying the body!

Similar to most beverages in this book, water kefir can undergo a secondary fermentation, which makes it fizzy. This beverage is known as kefir soda. Once the primary fermentation is complete, you are free to stop there and enjoy the water kefir, but flavoring water kefir for the secondary fermentation is fun and gives the naturally bubbly beverage a lot of spunk.

If you don't know anyone who makes water kefir, you will need to purchase dehydrated kefir grains. There are many reliable water grain sources on the Internet. To be effective for fermentation, dehydrated water kefir grains need to be rehydrated and activated. This process can take quite a while (one to three weeks), but once the grains are active, they can be used over and over again to make probiotic sodas.

Health Benefits of Water Kefir and Kefir Soda

Aside from its probiotic density, water kefir (and kefir soda) is a very hydrating beverage and is a great replacement for electrolyte sport drinks, as it contains enzymes and minerals. Water kefir helps reduce inflammation, thus easing any digestive discomfort and also helps relieve skin irritation such as eczema and acne. Drinking water kefir is also wonderful for detoxification, as the beverage helps clean out the liver.

Secondary Fermentation

After the water kefir is finished fermenting, you can either consume it immediately or add ingredients to allow it to go through a secondary fermentation. This process will generate kefir soda as long as there is ample added sugar (from fruit, fruit juice, or cane sugar) and/or fruit pulp, which will make the water kefir fizzy. Secondary fermentation for kefir soda takes between two and three days and results in a wonderfully effervescent beverage.

It is always wise to be careful when opening bottles after secondary fermentation, as pressure builds and liquid can fizz out. Be particularly careful if using flip-cap bottles because these bottles are so air-tight that they tend to seal pressure in almost too well. When opening a bottle of kefir soda, always point it away from your face and away from other people. I do not recommend handing a bottle of kefir soda to a child to open.

Flavoring Water Kefir or Turning it into Kefir Soda

Water kefir tastes the best when it is flavored. Without added ingredients, water kefir has a slightly sweet, lemony, and yeasty flavor, which can be an acquired taste. Adding fruit juices or whole fruit, herbs, or teas allows you to cater the flavors to your pallet. If you know you like sweeter beverages, be sure to add a little extra juice or fruit prior to sealing the bottles for secondary fermentation so that the probiotics have enough sugar to ferment a second time with some leftover sweetness for you to enjoy.

The easiest way of flavoring water kefir is by adding 100 percent pure juices prior to bottling it for secondary fermentation. About 1 cup of juice per 4 cups of water kefir provides good flavor and plenty of fizziness. It seems as though all probiotic drinks love fructose more than sucrose for secondary fermentation. Water kefir will become kefir soda and yield the fizziest results when fruit and/or fruit juice is added to it prior to secondary fermentation.

Important Precautions

Kefir grains react in a very adverse way to metals. For this reason, be sure to avoid metal touching water kefir liquid or grains at any time. When straining the water kefir to separate it from the grains, always use a fine plastic strainer, which can be purchased at most kitchen and home stores or online.

Use a glass jar or jug for fermenting the water kefir. Glass is easy to sanitize and it doesn't trap bacteria, chemicals, or BPA. You want to avoid anything contaminating your probiotic drink and the best way of doing so is to brew it in glass.

If at any time your water kefir smells rancid or similar to rotten milk, your batch has gone bad and, unfortunately, you need to start over with new grains. During the first day or two of fermentation, the liquid will not have much of a smell, and by the third or fourth day, it will smell lemony and yeasty. The odor should never be off-putting or foul, and as long as you follow the instructions carefully, you won't have a problem.

Like most probiotic beverages, water kefir prefers to be at room temperature to ferment, which is typically in the high-60s to mid-70s. The jar the water kefir is fermenting in should never feel warm to the touch—if it does feel warm, you run the risk of killing the probiotics.

Similar to bread yeast (or really any live culture), it is definitely possible to kill the water kefir culture if you use too much sugar in your sugar water solution. You may have the intention of giving the water kefir grains an extra boost or treat, but using more sugar than what is recommended in these recipes may result in your water kefir grains dying and/or killing the probiotics in the drink.

While you should keep the water kefir in a clean environment, you do not need to sanitize the jar the water kefir brews in between batches (the same is true for brewing kombucha and jun). As long as the culture you are brewing is healthy, the probiotics will prohibit bad bacteria from growing in the jar, which makes sanitizing it between batches unnecessary. Nevertheless, I do recommend cleaning the jar out every few batches for peace of mind, as slimy film will form on the edges of the jar. This is perfectly normal, but for safety purposes, a good cleaning with hot water and soap is recommended from time to time.

The instructions below describe how to make water kefir from start to finish, followed by recipes to make delicious probiotic soda flavors. We start by activating kefir grains, followed by making water kefir, and then allow the water kefir to go through secondary fermentation to turn it into a fizzy "soda."

Tools you need for making water kefir:

- 1 large glass jar (does not need to have a lid)
- Cheesecloth or a kitchen towel
- Stretchy rubber band
- Fine plastic strainer (preferably a small one, the size of the mouth of a glass)
- Dehydrated (or hydrated) water kefir grains

To activate dehydrated kefir grains:

1. Dissolve 1/3 cup of sugar in 4 cups of water. Allow the sugar water to cool to room temperature. Anything hotter than room temperature can kill the culture of bacteria and yeast.
2. Pour the sugar water into a glass jar along with the dehydrated kefir grains. Cover the jar with a cheesecloth or kitchen towel bound with a rubber band in order to keep bugs out. Place on the counter, in a pantry, or in a generally undisturbed area.
3. Allow this to sit for two to three days, no longer than five days.
4. Strain grains using a fine plastic strainer, discarding the liquid.
5. Repeat this process several times until the kefir grains are "active." You will know your kefir grains are active when the water they sit in becomes bubbly at the top and smells yeasty and lemony. At no point

should the liquid smell foul, like spoiled milk. If this occurs, discard both the batch of water kefir and the grains and start again with a new set of grains. Your grains should appear plump, somewhat translucent, will continue to grow, and will resemble small cauliflower florets.

Note:
The activation process truly can take several weeks. In fact, it took my dehydrated grains three weeks to activate. Yes, this means you will be pouring out batch after batch of sugar water to keep the grains fed and healthy. It will seem wasteful but it will be worth it once your grains are active and you can experiment with the recipes in this section!

To make water kefir:

1. Dissolve ½ cup of sugar in 10 cups of water.

2. Allow the sugar water to cool to room temperature. Pour it into a large glass jar or container, and then add in the activated kefir grains.

3. Cover the jar with cheesecloth or a dish towel secured by a rubber band.

4. Allow grains to sit for two to three days at room temperature. You may need to lengthen the fermentation time up to four days if your house is chilly, but never leave water kefir for longer than five days or your grains will starve. You will notice small bubbles rise from the bottom of the jar to the top and some foam or larger bubbles will settle on the surface of the liquid. The liquid will smell yeasty and almost lemony. These are all signs that your water kefir is ready!

5. Strain the liquid into a pitcher or into bottles to flavor it or drink plain.

6. You are now ready to bottle your first batch of water kefir and start a new batch using the same active water kefir grains. You can continue using the same grains an infinite number of times, as long as you keep them healthy!

To flavor the water kefir or make kefir soda:

1. Prepare a recipe from this section or add 100 percent pure fruit juice of your choice to water kefir (about 1 cup of fruit juice per 4 cups water kefir).

2. Bottle the liquid in an air-tight container.

3. Leave the bottles at room temperature for two to three days to allow secondary fermentation to take place.

4. Place bottles in the refrigerator to slow the fermentation. Note that the beverage will continue to ferment in the refrigerator. For best results, wait a full twenty-four hours before drinking the cooled kefir soda, as the longer you wait, the fizzier it will get.

Cherry Lime Soda

A surefire way of achieving a fizzy kefir soda is to add 100 percent pure fruit juice to it prior to bottling. The probiotics continue to ferment by feeding off the fructose, gas pressure builds up in the sealed bottles, and a carbonated drink results. Cherry is always a delicious choice for a fizzy beverage and cherries are full of nutrients! They contain a high density of anthocyanins, which are antioxidants that can prevent heart disease and cancer. Anthocyanins also act as an anti-inflammatory, which is good for maintaining healthy joints and can even help alleviate arthritis. Cherries are full of folate, magnesium, iron, potassium, as well as vitamins C & E! This superfruit is touted as a brain food, promoting information retention and memory. Mix the juice up with fresh squeezed lime juice and you have yourself a fizzy and tasty soda.

Ingredients:

- 2 cups 100% cherry juice
- 5 limes, juiced
- 8 cups water kefir (page 134)

Instructions:

1. Add all ingredients to a pitcher or jug and stir together.
2. Pour into sealable bottles and seal.
3. Leave bottles at room temperature for two to three days

Vanilla Water Kefir

If you have ever thought about making soda at home, you have probably happened upon the idea of making cream soda. While all you need is some sugar and vanilla paste to mimic the cream soda flavor, this beverage does not become fizzy, as water kefir seems to prefer fructose for becoming effervescent over sucrose. This beverage is enjoyable as is, or you can try adding your favorite juice in place of the sugar water to generate a fizzier fruity vanilla drink.

Ingredients:

- ½ cup water
- ½ cup sugar
- 3 teaspoons vanilla paste*
- 8 cups water kefir (page 134)

Instructions:

1. Dissolve the sugar in the water by heating it on the stove top in a saucepan. Once the sugar is incorporated, remove the saucepan from the heat and add the vanilla paste, stirring to incorporate.
2. Allow the vanilla mixture to cool completely by pouring it into a container and refrigerating until the temperature is lowered to room temperature (somewhere in the 70° Fahrenheit range).
3. Pour into sealable bottles and seal.
4. Secure the air-tight lids and leave the bottles at room temperature for two to three days for secondary fermentation.
5. Place bottles in the refrigerator to slow the fermentation.
6. Drink chilled and enjoy!

*Vanilla paste can be found at most natural food stores and is very similar to vanilla extract. You can replace the vanilla paste with 3 teaspoons pure vanilla extract or the scrapings from 3 vanilla beans.

Orange Ginger Soda

Citrus and fresh ginger make a fine pair. Ginger is phenomenal for easing nausea and calming stomach pain and is a natural antibiotic. Combining fresh orange juice and ginger with water kefir, which is already rich in probiotics, makes for a soothing, immunity-boosting elixir, which is wonderful any time of year and particularly great for soothing colds. This recipe results in a bubbly, flavorful kefir soda that is easy to make any time of year.

Ingredients:

- 3 cups orange juice (not from concentrate)
- 2 tablespoons fresh ginger, grated
- 8 cups water kefir (page 134)

Instructions:

1. Add all ingredients to a pitcher and stir well to combine.
2. Pour the Orange Ginger water kefir into sealable bottles and secure their lids.
3. Leave bottles at room temperature for three days to allow for secondary fermentation.
4. Place bottles in the refrigerator to slow fermentation and to chill for drinking.
5. When ready to drink, strain the liquid into a glass using a fine strainer to remove the ginger pulp.

Peach Soda

Peaches lend a soft and sweet flavor to kefir soda and the pulp helps the soda get very effervescent! After this beverage undergoes secondary fermentation, be very careful when opening the air-tight bottles, especially if they are flip-cap bottles. Pressure will build during secondary fermentation and may result in the soda fizzing over when opening if the bottles are left for too long at room temperature.

Ingredients:

- 2 large ripe peaches, peeled, pitted, and chopped
- ½ cup water
- ¼ cup sugar
- 8 cups water kefir (page 134)

Instructions:

1. Add chopped peaches and water to a small saucepan. Cover it and cook on medium until it comes to a full boil.

2. Reduce temperature to a gentle boil, leaving the pan covered until peaches lose their form entirely, about 30 minutes. Mash the peaches and stir the fruit occasionally to help the process and cook uncovered for the last 10 minutes to help reduce the mixture. You want the substance to be thick and fairly smooth, but a little chunkiness is okay.

3. Add the sugar and stir to dissolve. Remove the pan from heat and allow the peach mixture to cool to room temperature.

4. In a pitcher or jug, combine the peach mixture with the water kefir and stir well.

5. Pour into sealable bottles and leave the bottles sealed at room temperature for two to three days for secondary fermentation.

6. Place bottles in the refrigerator to stop the fermentation.

7. If your soda has small chunks of peaches or pulp, you can strain the beverage prior to drinking. Serve cold and enjoy!

Sarsaparilla Water Kefir

If you're a fan of root beer, you will adore making sarsaparilla water kefir at home! All you need is sarsaparilla root, which can be purchased from a natural food store, and you'll be on your way to root beer-flavored water kefir! Because water kefir becomes fizziest when using fruit juice or fresh fruit, this beverage does not become very fizzy, although there is some effervescence after it has completed secondary fermentation. While the drink won't have the carbonated feature of root beer, it will certainly taste like it!

Sarsaparilla roots contain saponin, which gives the root antibacterial and anti-inflammatory qualities. They also help ease digestive discomfort and purify the blood, making this root very useful for natural medicine.

Ingredients:

- 1 cup water
- ¼ cup sarsaparilla root
- ¼ cup sugar
- 4 cups water kefir (page 134)

Instructions:

1. Heat 1 cup of water in a saucepan until boiling. Add the sarsaparilla root and sugar and allow it to steep for at least 30 minutes.

2. Allow tea to cool to room temperature (or place in the refrigerator to get it to cool more quickly).

3. Combine the water kefir and sarsaparilla tea in a pitcher. Spoon the sarsaparilla root pulp into the bottles—the pulp will help with the secondary fermentation and continue to infuse flavor into the drink.

4. Pour mixture into sealable glass bottles.

5. Leave the bottles at room temperature for three days.

6. Place bottles in the refrigerator to chill.

7. When ready to drink, strain out the sarsaparilla roots with a fine strainer.

Raspberry Kefir Soda

Raspberry-flavored probiotic drinks are almost always crowd pleasers. You can either serve this beverage as water kefir immediately after preparing it, or you can bottle it in air-tight bottles and allow it to go through secondary fermentation for a few days to get raspberry soda.

Ingredients:

- 2 cups fresh raspberries
- ½ cup water
- ¼ cup sugar
- 8 cups water kefir (page 134)

Instructions:

1. Heat the raspberries, water, and sugar in a saucepan and bring it to a full boil.

2. Reduce heat and allow mixture to bubble for a couple of minutes.

3. Remove from heat and allow mixture to cool to room temperature. To speed up this process, pour raspberry mixture in a bowl and refrigerate until cooled.

4. Add raspberry mixture and water kefir to a pitcher and stir well.

5. Pour liquid (including raspberry pulp) into sealable bottles.

6. Seal the bottles and leave them at room temperature for two to three days for secondary fermentation. The longer they are left at room temperature, the fizzier the soda will get, so be careful to not leave the bottles for too long or else they will fizz over when opened.

7. Before drinking, strain out the raspberry pulp with a fine strainer.

Kefir Lemonade

While this book contains an entire section on probiotic lemonade, let's not forget we can make lemonade using kefir, too! This is a great introductory recipe for those who have never tried water kefir, as the lemon juice shines through as the dominant flavor and creates a refreshing drink. This easy-to-make recipe is perfect for those who are new to probiotic beverages and awesome for adolescents who don't have the taste for stronger beverages such as kombucha.

Note that this beverage does not become very effervescent, even after secondary fermentation. You can therefore serve it immediately after preparing it or bottle it and allow it to go through secondary fermentation to continue to feed the probiotics and yeasts.

Ingredients:

- ½ cup fresh lemon juice (about 4 lemons, squeezed)
- ¼ cup water
- ¼ cup sugar
- 8 cups water kefir (page 134)

Instructions:

1. Gently heat the lemon juice, water, and sugar in a saucepan just until sugar dissolves.
2. Allow mixture to cool to room temperature. To speed up this process, pour it into a container and refrigerate.
3. Combine the lemon and sugar mixture with the water kefir in a large pitcher or jug.
4. Pour into sealable containers.
5. Seal the bottles and leave them at room temperature for two to three days for secondary fermentation (or simply put the bottles straight into the refrigerator or serve immediately).
6. Refrigerate the kefir lemonade and enjoy chilled.

Milk Kefir

About Kefir

The more commonly known and consumed kefir is “milk kefir,” which can be purchased from most grocery stores in the yogurt section. While the exact origin of kefir is unknown, it is said that it was first made in the Caucasus Mountains by fermenting fresh cow milk with kefir grains inside pouches made of goat leather. The word “kefir” is Turkish for “good feeling” and is made by fermenting milk kefir grains in cow, goat, or coconut milk.

Milk kefir grains are not grains at all. They look like small cauliflower florets, which are the result of colonies of bacteria and yeast bonding together and growing. When milk kefir grains are fermented with milk, a tangy, thick substance similar to yogurt forms. Kefir is typically served in a glass as a beverage but one can also use it to make smoothies.

Kefir tends to be very expensive, so making kefir at home is a much more affordable (and healthy!) option than purchasing it. In this section, I have provided two options for making kefir. The first is by using freeze-dried kefir starter and the other (more authentic version) is by using milk kefir grains. Also in this section are recipes for making your kefir even more delicious!

You will also find recipes for water kefir (or kefir soda) in this cookbook. While water kefir and milk kefir are similar in the sense that they are both probiotic beverages, you cannot use water kefir grains to make milk kefir, nor can you use milk kefir grains to make water kefir.

Similar to making homemade yogurt, one can use store-bought plain kefir as starter for homemade kefir. More commonly, kefir is prepared using kefir grains or freeze-dried kefir, and instructions for both are provided in this section. When using cow’s milk, it doesn’t matter what the fat content is, although milk that is higher in fat results in a thicker, creamier, tangier, and sweeter kefir. When using coconut milk, the full-fat kind from the can is recommended.

When flavoring homemade kefir, various fresh ripe fruit and/or sweeteners can be used. Using in-season fruit and natural sweeteners results in a delicious, healthful beverage with a flavor you won’t find in store-bought kefir!

Kefir is full of essential vitamins and probiotics. It is dense in vitamins A, B1, B6, D, and folic acid. It is also stated that drinking kefir can help repair any damage that has been done to the stomach and intestinal lining. This is helpful to those who have frequent or occasional digestive problems or even disorders such as Crohn's disease, celiac disease, candida, or irritable bowl syndrome. Those who are lactose intolerant may still be able to drink kefir because the fermentation process results in the presence of lactase, which is the enzyme that helps humans digest milk.

It is possible to make kefir using coconut milk using milk kefir grains. Although the process is the same as making kefir with cow's milk, the kefir grains will need to be returned to regular milk periodically in order to keep them alive and well. To make dairy-free kefir, simply follow the same instructions outlined in Option 2, using coconut milk in place of cow's milk.

Option 1: Making Kefir Using Freeze-Dried Kefir Starter

Ingredients:

- 1 liter milk
- 5 grams freeze-dried kefir starter (1 packet)

You also need:

- 1 quart-sized jar or container
- Large pot for heating milk
- Thermometer
- Fine plastic strainer

Instructions:

1. Heat the milk in a large pot until it reaches 180°F. As the milk heats and becomes frothy, stir constantly. Do not allow the milk to boil.

2. Remove milk from heat and allow it to cool to 73° to 77°F. To speed up the process, you can put the pot on top of ice or put it in the refrigerator.

3. Pour 5 grams (1 packet) of freeze-dried kefir starter into a bowl. Pour a small amount of the cooled milk into the bowl with the starter. Mix to dissolve the starter, then pour it into the pot with the rest of the milk, stirring to incorporate.

4. Pour the kefir mixture into a quart-sized mason jar and cover it with cheesecloth, coffee filter, or dish towel bound with a rubber band. Leave at room temperature for twenty-four hours, until you can see curds have formed.

5. Refrigerate the kefir (this stops the culturing process).

6. When ready to consume, strain the kefir using a fine plastic strainer, as curds will have formed.

7. You are now ready to flavor your kefir if desired!

Notes:

1. *For a number of years, kefir experts have cautioned against using metal during any part of the kefir-making process and have suggested using wooden spoons for stirring and plastic strainers when straining. New research states it may be okay to use stainless steel instruments for making kefir, but definitely stay away from any other metals.*
2. *When your kefir is finished, you will end up with a thick and somewhat chunky kefir. This is normal. Simply strain the kefir (using a fine plastic strainer) before consuming it for a creamy result.*

Option 2: Making Kefir using Kefir Grains

Ingredients:

- 2 tablespoons milk kefir grains
- 2 cups milk

Instructions:

1. You will first need to rehydrate your milk kefir grains if they are dehydrated. Follow the instructions your milk kefir supplier gives you to hydrate them. This process will be similar to simply making milk kefir.

2. Once kefir grains are active and hydrated, simply add them to a jar and pour milk on top. Cover with a cheesecloth, coffee filter, or dish towel bound by a rubber band.

3. Allow jar to sit at room temperature (70° to 78° Fahrenheit is best). If the room the kefir is in is cooler, it will take longer to culture. If the room is hotter, the kefir will culture faster for twenty-four hours.

4. Using a fine plastic strainer, strain the milk kefir grains over a jar, separating the kefir from the kefir grains.

5. Refrigerate the kefir to chill it and start a new batch of kefir with your milk kefir grains!

Note:
Two tablespoons of grains for every 2 cups of milk is standard, although the kefir grains will grow over time, so you can make larger batches as the kefir grains grow.

TROUBLESHOOTING:

If you allow your kefir to sit for longer than twenty-four hours, it may separate. Your kefir has separated if there is a clear but cloudy substance at the bottom of the jar and large chunks have risen to the top. This is still drinkable, though it may not be as pleasant as kefir that is still in its creamy state. If your kefir has separated, you do not need to throw away your milk kefir grains. You may still use them.

LAIT PUR DE NORMANDIE
ARRIVAGE 2 FOIS PAR JOUR
Le bon lait
31-29-73-46
Ferme du Vallon

Maple Chai Kefir

Milky, sweet chai tea is great any time of year and is particularly enjoyable when the weather cools down. Incorporating the warm chai tea flavors into this cold beverage makes kefir desirable even during the fall and winter when most of us crave hot drinks. To get pristine chai flavors, you can either make your own chai spice at home using spices you probably already have, or you can purchase chai spice from the grocery store. The maple syrup used to naturally sweeten this drink adds great flavor richness and pure maple syrup is great for you! It has both manganese and zinc, which play essential roles in the immune system and men's reproductive health.

Ingredients:

- 1½ to 2 tablespoons 100% pure maple syrup
- 1 teaspoon chai spice (see recipe below)
- 3 cups plain homemade kefir (pages 151–154)

Homemade Chai Spice:

- 2 teaspoons ground cinnamon
- 1 teaspoon ground cardamom
- 1 teaspoon ground ginger
- ½ teaspoon ground nutmeg
- ¼ teaspoon ground cloves
- Pinch black pepper

Use extra homemade chai spice for baked goods, adding to hot chocolate or coffee, or for flavoring kombucha, jun, or yogurt!

Instructions:

Combine all ingredients for the Maple Chai in a pitcher and mix well, ensuring the spices are evenly distributed. You can also blend all of the ingredients together in a blender.

Notes:
You can also make this recipe into Vanilla Chai by scraping the insides of one vanilla bean and mixing it in with the rest of the ingredients.

Keeps in the refrigerator for up to 5 days. Stir before drinking.

Mango Kefir

Similar to a mango lassi, this mango kefir is a very drinkable and enjoyable beverage. Sweet, ripe mangos give the drink an exotic and unique feel. Ripe mangos can be found at the grocery store during most months of the year, making this a convenient go-to beverage. Aside from the fact that mangos taste great, they are also very nutritious. They are full of vitamins C and A and also contain antioxidant compounds and enzymes that help prevent leukemia, prostate cancer, and breast cancer. Mangos also work to clear skin pores, making them a natural treatment for acne when consumed or used topically.

Ingredients:

- 1 ripe mango, peeled, pitted, and chopped (about 1 cup)
- 2 teaspoons agave nectar, optional
- 2 cups kefir (pages 151–154)

Instructions:

Add the three ingredients to a blender and blend until smooth. As an alternative, you can blend the mango and agave together (separate from the kefir) in a high-powered blender and serve it on top of plain kefir for a layered treat!

Note:
Keeps in the refrigerator for up to five days. Stir well before drinking.

Key Lime Kefir

How about key lime pie in a glass? That's how this kefir tastes with sweet, creamy, zesty flavor. Key limes are much smaller than regular limes and have a more tart and slightly sweet flavor. They also have far less juice than regular limes, but don't let the time it takes to juice the key limes deter you, as the beverage is well worth all the squeezing!

Ingredients:

- 1½ tablespoons key lime juice (about 8 to 10 key limes)
- 1 tablespoon sugar*
- ⅓ cup coconut milk
- 1 cup kefir (pages 151–154)

*Sugar can be replaced with agave nectar to taste. If using agave, simply combine all ingredients together and skip step 1 in the instructions.

Instructions:

1. In a saucepan, heat coconut milk, key lime juice, and sugar just until sugar dissolves. Pour mixture into a cup and place in the refrigerator until cooled completely.
2. Combine all ingredients in a cup and stir well to combine.

Note:
Keeps in the refrigerator for up to five days.

Cranberry Kefir

Given all of the amazing health benefits of cranberries, it's a wonder we don't eat them more often! They are high in Vitamin C and contain almost as much antioxidant density as blueberries. Cranberries are known to prevent bacteria from attaching to the urinary tract, helping to guard against and relieve urinary tract infections.

Cranberries are easy to find year-round, as good quality frozen cranberries are available when fresh ones are not. Due to the tart nature of cranberries, this recipe requires some extra sweetness to counterbalance the acidity, which can be achieved using agave nectar or honey to make a naturally sweetened beverage.

Ingredients:

- 2 cups fresh or frozen cranberries
- 2 tablespoons sugar
- ¼ cup water
- 2 cups plain homemade kefir (pages 151–154)

Instructions:

1. Heat the cranberries, water, and sugar in a small saucepan, covered over medium heat.
2. Cook until cranberries are softened, juices are seeping out, and the berries begin to lose their form when mashed with a fork.
3. Pour the cranberry mixture into a glass and refrigerate until completely cooled.
4. Place cranberry mixture in a blender with kefir and blend until smooth and combined.

Note:
Keeps in the refrigerator for up to five days.

Chocolate Kefir

Chocolate kefir is a decadent treat and a great change up from the fruit-flavored kefir. In spite of this recipe being more dessert-like in nature, it too has health benefits! Raw cacao powder is one of the world's natural super foods. It is chocolate in its raw form before oils, milks, and sugars have been added to it. Cacao powder contains antioxidants, which slow and prevent damage to your cells. It also affects the adrenal system and pleasure receptors to illicit happiness and even increases metabolism. While you can turn this into a naturally sweetened recipes using agave, sugar seems to work best from a flavor and textural standpoint.

Ingredients:

- ½ cup milk
- 2 tablespoons raw cacao powder*
- 3 tablespoons sugar
- 2 cups kefir (pages 151–154)

*raw cacao powder can be replaced with cocoa powder, but the flavor will be different.

Instructions:

1. Add the milk, cacao powder, and sugar to a small saucepan and heat over medium. Stir constantly to dissolve the sugar and cacao powder and don't allow the mixture to come to a boil. Once the mixture is completely combined and there are no more chunks of cacao powder, remove it from heat and allow it to cool. You can speed up this process by pouring it into a cup and refrigerating.

2. Strain 2 cups of kefir into a glass or jar.

3. Once cool, combine the chocolate mixture with the kefir and stir until both substances are combined.

Note:
Keeps in the refrigerator for up to five days.

Peach & Honey Kefir

Peaches and kefir are a match made in heaven. It is no mystery that peaches go well with just about anything creamy because it provides a wonderful sweet and tart counterbalance. This is an incredibly easy recipe, involving only three ingredients plus a blender. The honey enhances the flavor of the peaches and, because this is a naturally sweetened beverage, it is nothing but healthy (and delicious)!

Ingredients:

- 3 ripe peaches, chopped
- 2 tablespoons honey
- 2 cups kefir (pages 151–154)

Instructions:

1. Peel, pit, and chop the peaches.
2. Add the peaches and honey to high-powered blender. Blend until completely smooth. If necessary, add a tablespoon of water to help blend the peaches.
3. Add in homemade kefir that has been strained and blend until smooth.

Note:
Keeps in the refrigerator for up to five days.

Strawberry Kefir

Strawberry kefir is a wonderful beverage to have on hand at any given time. It is easy to make in a large batch, is a winner for just about anyone, and can be easily incorporated into your favorite fruit smoothies. To make this a naturally sweetened beverage, use agave nectar, maple syrup, or even date sugar in place of cane sugar. For those trying to introduce their children to kefir, this is the perfect recipe!

Ingredients:

- 4 cups kefir (pages 151–154)
- 4 cups fresh strawberries, chopped
- ¼ cup sugar or agave nectar

Instructions:

1. Add chopped strawberries to a saucepan, cover, and heat over medium.

2. Allow mixture to come to a full boil and continue to cook until juices are seeping out, bubbling, and strawberries are softened, about 10 minutes.

3. Add the sugar and stir to dissolve.

4. Remove from heat and allow mixture to cool slightly before pouring it into a bowl or container. Refrigerate strawberry mixture until completely cold.

5. Add kefir and strawberry mixture to a blender and blend until smooth. Serve immediately or store in a sealed container.

Note:
Keeps in the refrigerator for up to five days.

Roasted Banana Kefir

For those who have never tried roasted bananas, I highly recommend them! The roasting process brings out the natural sweetness of bananas and gives them a rich and almost caramel-like flavor. It doesn't take long at all to roast bananas and the flavor is so different from raw bananas, it is well worth the extra step! This beverage comes out thick and tastes like a decadent treat, but it is nothing but healthy for you, as it is naturally sweetened with honey. This is a great kefir flavor to add to smoothies (or even a milkshake!), giving the smoothie a completely unique and ultra sweet and creamy flavor.

Ingredients:

- 2 ripe (but firm) bananas
- 2 tablespoons honey
- 2 cups plain homemade kefir (pages 151–154)

Instructions:

1. Preheat the oven to 400° Fahrenheit.
2. Peel the bananas and slice them down the middle, length-wise.
3. Place a piece of aluminum foil in a casserole dish and put the bananas on top of the foil. Drizzle honey on top of the bananas.
4. Bake bananas in the oven for 10 to 12 minutes until they have browned slightly.
5. Remove from the oven and allow bananas to cool to room temperature (or place them in the refrigerator to cool all the way).
6. Place bananas and kefir in a blender and blend until completely smooth.
7. Serve immediately or chill and drink within twenty-four hours. Do not save this recipe more than a day or two as the bananas will continue to oxidize and the flavor won't be as good as when it is served fresh.

Note:
Keeps in the refrigerator for up to five days.

Blueberry Kefir

Blueberries are available fresh throughout the majority of the year, making this an easy kefir flavor during virtually any season. Blueberries are full of antioxidants and are said to be one of the world's greatest super foods, a wonderful "brain" food, and provide a high density of vitamins. Although it is recommended to make any recipe in this book using fresh fruit, blueberries can always be found in the frozen fruit section, making this a convenient flavor for a quick fix.

Ingredients:

- 2 cup fresh or frozen blueberries
- 1 tablespoon water
- 1 tablespoon sugar or agave nectar
- 2 cups plain homemade kefir (pages 151–154)

Instructions:

1. Add the blueberries and water to a saucepan and cook over medium heat, covered.

2. Once the juices are seeping out of the blueberries and bubbling, add the sugar (or agave) and stir to dissolve.

3. Lower the heat slightly and cook another 3 minutes.

4. Remove from heat and pour the blueberry mixture into a sealable container. Place in the refrigerator until completely cool.

5. Strain 2 cups of homemade kefir into a blender and add the blueberry mixture. Blend until completely smooth.

Note:
Keeps in the refrigerator for up to five days.

Yogurt

About Yogurt

Yogurt is cultured milk, a process whereby bacteria eats the milk lactose and converts it into lactic acid. Lactic acid reacting with milk protein thickens the milk, creating a sweet, tangy, creamy substance. Yogurt is traditionally fermented using cow's milk, but non-dairy yogurts can be made using soy, coconut, or almond milks. The exact origin of yogurt is unknown, but there are mentions of it in ancient Turkish and Indian texts. Each culture has its own traditional take on how yogurt should taste, what type of animal's milk to use, as well as the preferred thickness of the yogurt. Many cultures use yogurt in savory meals as well as sweet treats.

While yogurt is technically not a beverage, it is fitting for this book in the sense that it can be blended with other ingredients and made into smoothies or lassis. Check out the smoothie recipes that use homemade yogurt starting on page 203.

Health Benefits of Yogurt

Similar to all the probiotic beverages in this book, the list of the health benefits of yogurt seems to go on forever. The probiotics in yogurt help keep a healthy balance of microflora in your gut, which helps create regularity in your digestive system, relieving both constipation and diarrhea and helping food move along your digestive tract. Yogurt can also help prevent colon cancer and relieve irritable bowel syndrome. Women who struggle with candida can be prone to vaginal yeast infections, and consuming yogurt regularly can help to prevent these infections.

Yogurt contains protein (12 grams per cup!), magnesium, zinc, potassium, calcium, riboflavin, and vitamins B6 and B12. A breakfast or snack consisting of yogurt with fruit, nuts or granola, honey, or maple syrup is a delicious and healthful treat.

Yogurt is easier for our bodies to digest than milk. Through the fermentation process of yogurt, the probiotics create lactase, which is an enzyme that helps break down lactose, the sugar in milk. People who are lactose-intolerant have low levels of lactase, which makes it difficult for them to digest dairy products. Because the probiotics in dairy have eaten a portion of the lactose and yielded lactase, some people who are lactose-intolerant can enjoy yogurt without getting sick.

If you're going to buy yogurt from the store, be careful which brands you choose. Not all yogurt contains live and active cultures (meaning there are no beneficial probiotics), so be sure to read the labels and check which ones contain live cultures prior to purchasing. In addition, some brands add more cane sugar, stabilizers, and preservatives than others. Making yogurt at home ultimately results in a live, probiotic-rich food that can be flavored according to your tastes and nutritional needs.

Making Yogurt at Home

How to sanitize jars

It is important to properly sanitize the vessels you use for storing yogurt to ensure there are no harmful bacteria on them before you pour in the yogurt base. Yogurt cultures at a temperature that is optimal for all types of bacteria to grow—both good and bad. Because you are providing a desirable environment for bacteria growth, you want to be sure the only bacteria present are the probiotics.

You can either hand wash the jugs or jars you use for storing the yogurt with hot soapy water, or fill them with boiling water and allow them to sit for a few minutes, or you can sanitize canning jars by following the instructions below.

1. Place the jars mouth-side up, along with the lids and screw tops, in a large pot and fill the pot with a few inches of water.
2. Cover the pot and bring it to a full boil. Boil the jars for 10 minutes.
3. Remove the pot from the stove and leave it covered until you are ready to fill them.

The advantage to using canning jars is the yogurt will last for a month when properly sealed. You can use various glass containers for storing the yogurt as long as it has a sealable lid; however, large (1-quart or 2-quart) canning jars seem to work the best.

Milk Fat Content

Yogurt can be made just as easily using 0%, 1%, 2%, or whole milk. Choosing the milk fat content of your yogurt is entirely up to your personal preference. The higher the fat content, the thicker and creamier the yogurt will be. You can make a non-fat or low-fat yogurt thicker by straining it with a cheesecloth, thus making it into Greek yogurt (see instructions for Greek yogurt, page 181).

Many people have the misconception that the lower the fat in food, the healthier it is. Studies show this is not always the case. Healthy fats (such as grass-fed animal protein or omega fats) help your digestive system process food properly; a diet void of fat causes digestive problems and inadequate nutrient absorption. With milk in particular, removing the fat also removes the vitamins and nutrients, which is why we have vitamin-fortified milks. While whole milk contains more calories than non-fat, milk fat (and fats in general) slows down the release of sugar into our blood stream, which lowers the amount of body fat that can be stored.

Milk fat content is pertinent to this section because it affects the end product of your homemade yogurt. The flavor, texture, and consistency are all different depending on the milk you use. My preference is whole milk yogurt and Greek yogurt. Greek yogurt can be made using both whole milk and lower fat milks to achieve a thicker consistency. Using thicker yogurt when following the recipes in this book is crucial, as the recipes will not turn out as well when made with thin yogurt. Not that whole milk yogurt and Greek yogurt are both thick, but Greek yogurt is thicker and also much tangier. For this reason, recipes made with Greek yogurt may require a small amount of additional sweetener depending on your preference.

Each yogurt recipe in this section was made with whole milk yogurt or Greek yogurt. Because both types of yogurt are thick, they provide a great base for adding additional ingredients that have liquid in them without compromising thick and creamy texture. Greek yogurt is strained of whey (the liquid in yogurt), which makes it the most optimal foundation for flavored yogurts. Please remember if you try any of the recipes in this section using a lower fat homemade yogurt (that hasn't been strained into Greek yogurt), it will likely turn out soupy. It will still taste great, but the texture will not be as thick and creamy.

A Note About Sweeteners

When flavoring homemade yogurt, you have a bounty of options for sweeteners. There are many sources of natural sweeteners that I recommend as substitutes for cane sugar if you prefer less processed, lower glycemic foods. I used cane sugar and agave in most of these recipes with the understanding that not everyone is in the habit of using all-natural sweeteners. Examples of great natural sweeteners are: agave nectar, maple syrup, honey (raw is always best), powdered honey, chopped dates, date sugar, coconut sugar, stevia, or xylitol. Simply combining maple syrup or sliced fruit with plain yogurt makes a healthful, wonderful snack.

Sweeteners that are in dehydrated or crystallized form (such as cane sugar, coconut sugar, date sugar, etc.), will need to be dissolved prior to adding it to the yogurt or you'll end up with a grainy, sour yogurt. To do so, simply heat all of the ingredients that are to be added to the yogurt on the stovetop and let the mixture cool completely before combining it with the yogurt.

Should you choose to use natural sweeteners that are in syrup form, such as agave, maple syrup, or honey, you can bypass the heating process for the fruit-based yogurt recipes and simply mash everything together; however, heating the fruit brings out its natural juices and creates a flavor that is difficult to mimic by leaving the fruit raw. For this reason, I still recommend following the instructions as specified in each recipe, even if you are using a liquid or syrup sweetener.

Some folks prefer their yogurt as tart as can be, whereas some people enjoy a sweeter yogurt. Depending on your individual tastes, consider adding or scaling back on the sweeteners. Most of these recipes were concocted using Greek yogurt, which is much more tart than regular yogurt and requires extra sweetening.

Yogurt and Smoothies (and Cooking)!

Yogurt is excellent in cooking and baking! For sauces that are typically mayonnaise-based, I always substitute the mayonnaise for plain yogurt or Greek yogurt. I love making fun, fancy hamburger sauces or fruit salads using yogurt! In addition, yogurt makes a great baking buddy. You can add it to pancake batter in place of milk and also use it in cakes, muffins, and breads. Never be worried about making too much yogurt at home, because you can always find other culinary uses for it!

Shelf Life of Homemade Yogurt

When properly sealed in a sanitized jar, plain yogurt can last for up to one month! After adding ingredients to the yogurt for flavor, the yogurt is best when used within one week. While the recipes in this book would likely last longer than one week, the flavors and textures are always best when consumed soon after the recipe is prepared.

When fruit is added to homemade yogurt, it tends to sink to the bottom of the container it is in, along with any liquid. Stir yogurt well before consuming for the best results.

Homemade Yogurt

Ingredients:

- Half gallon milk (2 quarts)*
- 1/3 cup whole milk plain yogurt (or Greek yogurt)**

*You can use anything from 0% milk fat to whole milk. Whole milk will make a much thicker and creamier yogurt, whereas nonfat milk yields a runnier yogurt.
**You can either use store-bought plain yogurt or homemade yogurt. If you use store-bought, make sure somewhere on the package there's a note indicating there are active and live cultures in the yogurt.

Instructions:

1. Pour milk in a large pot and heat just above medium, stirring every once in a while. The purpose of heating the milk is to kill any bad bacteria and also denature the milk proteins. Denaturing the proteins lends itself to the creamy texture of the yogurt, as without this process, curds would form instead of a creamy consistency.

2. As the milk heats, it will get frothy and bubbly—at this point, begin stirring the milk consistently. Use a thermometer to check the temperature of the milk. You want to heat the milk to 180° to 185° Fahrenheit and keep it at this temperature for a couple of minutes (you may need to reduce the heat on the stove as the milk gets closer to the optimal temperature). Do not allow the milk to boil.

3. Remove the pot from the heat and allow the milk to cool to between 115° to 120°. This is the optimal temperature range for allowing the probiotics to culture. Anything much hotter than 120 degrees will kill the probiotics. To speed up the cooling process, you can use an ice bath by placing the pot of milk in a larger pot with ice water, stirring occasionally. During the cooling process, skin will form on top of the milk, which you can either pull off with a spoon/fork or strain off with a fine metal strainer. Either way, getting rid of the skin will make the yogurt's texture more uniform.

4. Once milk has cooled to desired temperature, pour the store-bought yogurt into a bowl and add a small amount of the warm milk (a cup or two works great) and whisk together. Pour this mixture into the pot with the rest of the warm milk and stir together.

5. Pour the mixture into two 1-quart jars (or one 2-quart jar).

6. If there are any bubbles at the tops of the jars (likely there will be), scoop them out with a spoon before sealing the jars to achieve a creamier yogurt texture. You can also leave the lids off and cover the jars with cheesecloth secured with a rubber band. Both methods work.

7. Place jars in a pot filled with hot tap water (water should be between 120° and 125°F). Cover the pot. If your house is cold, wrap the pot in a blanket or towel and add more hot water as it begins to cool down. Allow the yogurt to sit at least 5 hours and up to 8 hours in a warm, dark spot. The longer the yogurt sits, the thicker and more tart it becomes.

8. The yogurt is ready when it is thick and smells like yogurt! When you refrigerate the yogurt, it will set up and become slightly thicker, so for best results, make sure you refrigerate the yogurt prior to consuming it.

9. Use the recipes in this section to flavor your yogurt, and have fun!

Homemade Greek Yogurt

Ingredients:

- 1 quart (32 ounces) homemade yogurt (see instructions beginning on page 179)*

*You can use homemade yogurt with any milk fat content, but whole milk yogurt turns out the thickest and creamiest.

You also need:

- A large bowl
- 1 large piece of cheesecloth
- 2 to 3 rubber bands

Instructions:

1. Fold a cheesecloth over onto itself (doubling its thickness) and lay it on top of a large bowl.

2. Pour yogurt onto the cheesecloth.

3. Take all of the edges of the cheesecloth and bring them together so that you have a bundle of yogurt. Use a rubber band to secure the cheesecloth around the yogurt completely.

4. Once you have your bundle secured, use one or two additional rubber bands to hang it from a cabinet or shelf over the mixing bowl so that the gravity helps drain the whey (liquid) from the yogurt.

5. Allow the yogurt to strain for 45 minutes to an hour.

6. Release the yogurt bundle from its rubber band hold and open up the cheesecloth. The yogurt should look thick and kind of stringy. Congratulations, you have just made Greek yogurt at home!

7. You know all of that whey you strained off of the yogurt? Don't throw it away! It is full of probiotics, and you can make lacto-fermented lemonade out of it! Head over to the lacto-fermented lemonade section of this book starting on page 89.

Coconut Milk Yogurt (Non-Dairy)

Ingredients:

- 2 13.5-ounce cans full fat coconut milk
- 1 6-ounce container of store-bought plain coconut milk yogurt

Instructions:

1. Pour the coconut milk into a medium to large-sized saucepan and heat until it reaches 180° Fahrenheit. Don't let the milk boil.
2. Remove from heat and allow the coconut milk to cool to between 110° and 115°F. Whisk in the 6 ounces of coconut milk yogurt.
3. Pour the substance into a quart-sized jar (or smaller pint-sized jars). Seal the jars with their lids.
4. Place the jar in a pot of hot water, making sure the water is around 120° to 125°F.
5. Allow the yogurt to ferment for 9 hours.

Note:
If you desire thicker yogurt, you may follow the steps outlined in the Greek yogurt section to strain it using cheese cloth.

Banana Cream Pie Yogurt

Banana Cream Pie Yogurt is one of my favorite yogurt recipes in this book, and also one of the quickest to prepare. It tastes so close to banana cream pie filling, but in contrast to banana cream pies, this yogurt is healthy. The coconut milk really brings out the "cream" part of this recipe, adding richness, although this yogurt is delicious without the coconut milk as well.

Because bananas oxidize very quickly and their flavor changes along with oxidation, it is best to eat this yogurt on the same day it is made. While other yogurt recipes in this book can easily be doubled or tripled to keep the flavor on hand, I recommend only making what will be consumed quickly, lest you end up with brown yogurt that has the flavor or overly ripe bananas. This recipe comes together in seconds and is delicious by itself or with granola or even on top of hot oatmeal!

Ingredients:

- 1 cup Greek yogurt (page 181)
- 1 ripe banana
- 2 tablespoons coconut milk (full-fat kind recommended)
- 2 teaspoons agave nectar or honey (or to taste)

Instructions:

1. In a bowl, mash the ripe banana.
2. Mix in the coconut milk and agave, stirring well to combine.
3. Add the yogurt and mix until combined.
4. Serve soon after preparing (banana will oxidize and turn brown if stored in the refrigerator for more than half a day).
5. Enjoy the yogurt by itself or with granola or on top of hot oatmeal.

Mojito Yogurt

Using cocktails, such as the mint mojito, as inspiration for flavoring homemade yogurt is fun and unique. This mojito yogurt includes lime juice and mint leaves just like the mojito cocktail, giving it a cool, zesty, and refreshing flavor. This yogurt can be made any time of year, but it is particularly great in the summer time. It can be eaten as is or blended with frozen cantaloupe to make the Cantaloupe Cooler from the smoothies section of this book (page 219).

Ingredients:

- 2 cup whole milk or Greek yogurt (page 179 or 181)
- 10 mint leaves, finely chopped (about 1 tablespoon)
- Zest of 1 lime
- 1 tablespoon lime juice
- 2 tablespoon agave nectar (or sugar)
- 1/3 cup coconut milk

Instructions:

1. Add the coconut milk, mint leaves, agave, lime juice, and zest to a small saucepan.
2. Heat over medium until it reaches a boil.
3. Reduce heat and simmer for 2 minutes.
4. Remove saucepan from heat and allow the mixture to cool for 10 minutes.
5. Using a small strainer, strain the mint leaves from the mixture and discard them.
6. Refrigerate the mojito mixture until chilled. The mixture should be fairly thick.
7. Once cool, combine the yogurt and mojito mixture.
8. Enjoy plain, turn it into frozen yogurt, or use it for the Cantaloupe Cooler in the smoothie section of this book.

Note:
Keeps in the refrigerator for up to one week.

Mocha Yogurt

While fruit-filled yogurt is tasty and healthful, we deserve a treat from time to time! Coffee lovers beware: this may be the new way by which you get your caffeine fix. This decadent mocha flavored yogurt is easy to make using coffee that you have already brewed. The yogurt can be enjoyed on its own or used for the Chocolate Protein Smoothie from the smoothie section in this book (page 211).

Ingredients:

- 2 cups Greek yogurt (page 181)
- 1/3 cup strong brewed coffee
- 4 tablespoons cocoa powder
- 2 tablespoons sugar (or to taste)

Instructions:

1. Add the cocoa powder and sugar to a small bowl.
2. Pour three tablespoons of hot strong-brewed coffee in the bowl and mix until the cocoa powder and sugar have completely dissolved and you have a thick, dark mixture.
3. Refrigerate the mixture until chilled.
4. Combine the yogurt and the mocha mixture and enjoy plain, with granola, or add to a Chocolate Protein Smoothie.

Note:
Keeps in the refrigerator for up to one week.

Vanilla Bean & Honey Yogurt

Vanilla yogurt tends to be a favorite for many households. It is versatile and appealing no matter the time of year. Because vanilla yogurt is a great one to keep in a large quantity, I provided a recipe for a quart-sized portion. The combination of vanilla and honey tastes great and the fact that this recipe is naturally sweetened makes it a healthful yogurt.

Not only does this yogurt taste great on its own, but it is wonderful for making fruit and granola parfaits as well as using in sweet baking or cooking recipes in place of milk. Adding a portion of yogurt to pancake batter along with some milk makes the pancakes thick, creamy, and slightly tangy.

Ingredients:

For 1 quart:

- 1 quart (4 cups) whole milk or Greek yogurt (page 179 or 181)
- 2 vanilla beans, scraped
- ¼ to ⅓ cup honey

Instructions:

1. Cut the vanilla bean in half, then slice each half open lengthwise.
2. Carefully scrape the tiny black vanilla beans out and into the yogurt. Stir well to integrate into the yogurt.
3. Pour honey in with the yogurt and stir quickly to incorporate.

Note:
If your honey is crystallized and/or not runny because your house is cold, you can heat it in a saucepan or in the microwave to get it to a runny consistency. Be sure to let it cool to room temperature before adding it to the yogurt.

Keeps in the refrigerator for up to two weeks.

Blueberry Yogurt

The tart and sweet flavors of fresh blueberries combined with creamy yogurt makes this recipe a no-brainer. This is a yogurt that most people (including small children!) will enjoy. Did you know blueberries are known as a brain food and can help improve memory? For this reason, it is said that eating blueberries prior to a big exam will help retain information. The antioxidants and vitamins in blueberries make the yogurt nutrient-dense and the fact that the recipe is naturally sweetened using agave makes it nothing but great for you.

Ingredients:

- 1½ cups fresh blueberries
- 2 tablespoons water
- 1 tablespoon agave nectar*
- 2 cups plain Greek yogurt (page 181)

*You can replace the agave with cane sugar, making sure to dissolve the sugar with the blueberries.

Instructions:

1. Add blueberries and water to a saucepan and heat over medium, covered.
2. Bring to a full boil and cook until blueberries are puffy and juices are seeping out. Remove the cover and allow some of the liquid to cook off so that the mixture becomes thicker, about 3 to 5 minutes.
3. Add agave nectar (or sugar), stir to combine and remove mixture from heat.
4. Pour blueberry mixture into a bowl or container. Refrigerate until completely cold.
5. In a bowl, mix together the yogurt and blueberry mixture until well combined.
6. Enjoy the yogurt by itself, with granola, or in a fruit smoothie!

Note:
Keeps in the refrigerator for up to one week.Stir well before consuming.

Raspberry Yogurt

Raspberry yogurt has always been one of my personal favorites, and there's nothing better than making it homemade. Raspberries are high in antioxidants, vitamin C, manganese, and fiber. Plus, studies show there are phytonutrients in raspberries that heat up fat cells, thereby stimulating the metabolism of fat. Raspberries add a colorful balance of sweet and tart flavors for a homemade treat that is worlds above store-bought yogurt.

Ingredients:

- 1½ cups fresh ripe raspberries
- 2 tablespoons water
- 1 tablespoon agave or sugar (or to taste)
- 2 cups whole milk or Greek yogurt (page 179 or 181)

Instructions:

1. Heat the raspberries and water at medium in a saucepan, covered.

2. After a couple of minutes, juices from the raspberries will seep out. Allow the mixture to come to a full boil. Remove the lid and allow some of the liquid to cook off to create a thicker mixture. Add the agave or sugar (making sure to dissolve the sugar completely) and then remove from heat. You can leave the raspberries whole or mash them with a fork depending on what kind of texture you want for your yogurt.

3. Pour the raspberry mixture into a bowl or container and place in the refrigerator until completely cold.

4. Combine the yogurt and raspberry mixture, stirring well to combine.

Note:
After this yogurt sits in the refrigerator, the agave and fruit may settle at the bottom, so stir the yogurt before eating.

Keeps in the refrigerator for up to two weeks.

Apple Cinnamon Yogurt

The fall and winter months are all about baking warmly spiced treats like the all-American favorite, apple pie! This recipe involves caramelizing apples in brown sugar with cinnamon, releasing rich, sweet, tart flavors. And if that doesn't sound comforting and cozy enough, combining the cooled caramelized apples with thick yogurt adds a creaminess resembling whipped cream. Should we call this "Apple Pie Yogurt?" I think so!

Ingredients:

- 3 cups whole milk or Greek yogurt (page 179 or 181)
- 3 apples (golden delicious recommended), peeled and chopped into small (1/2") pieces
- 2 tablespoons water, separated
- Pinch of salt
- 3 tablespoons brown sugar
- ½ teaspoon ground cinnamon
- ½ teaspoon pure vanilla extract
- Walnuts for serving

Instructions:

1. Add the chopped apples, cinnamon, 1 tablespoon of water, and a pinch of salt to a medium-sized saucepan.

2. Heat apples over medium heat, covered, stirring every couple of minutes. The apples will begin to boil and juices will seep out.

3. After about 10 minutes, add the brown sugar, the other tablespoon of water, and reduce heat to low. Continue to cook, covered, until apples lose most of their form and caramelize, about 8 to 10 minutes. If the apples begin to stick to the saucepan, add more water 1 tablespoon at a time. Some pieces of apples will retain a bit of form, which adds great texture to the yogurt!

4. Once apples are finished cooking, add the vanilla extract, stir, and remove from heat.

5. Allow the apple mixture to cool, then pour it into a container and refrigerate until completely cool.

6. In a mixing bowl, mix 1 quart of homemade yogurt and the apple mixture together.

7. Serve with chopped walnuts on top.

Note:
Keeps in the refrigerator for up to one week. Stir well before consuming.

Caramelized Pear & Cardamom Yogurt

Just like the Apple Cinnamon Yogurt in this section, Pear & Cardamom yogurt is a sweet and warmly spiced recipe, perfect for the fall and winter months. Cardamom is a spice commonly used in pumpkin and apple pies and adds a very unique flavor. Cardamom and pears are well-matched ingredients, making this a lovely yogurt that you won't find at the market.

Ingredients:

- 1 quart whole milk or Greek yogurt (page 179 or 181)
- 3 ripe bosc pears
- ¼ to ⅓ cup water
- 1 teaspoon lemon juice
- Dash salt
- ½ teaspoon cardamom
- 3 tablespoons agave nectar (or to taste)

Instructions:

1. Peel and chop the pears into small ¼" to ½" sized pieces.
2. Add the chopped pears to a small saucepan with about 2 tablespoons of water, the lemon juice, salt, and the cardamom.
3. Cook pears, covered, over medium heat. After about 5 minutes, add another couple tablespoons of water and continue cooking.
4. Cook until pears are softened and caramelized, leaving the saucepan covered and stirring every couple of minutes. This process should take 20 to 30 minutes.
5. If at any time the pears begin to stick to the bottom of the saucepan, add a little more water. The topping is finished when the pears are softened but still hold their form and there is a little bit of thick, sweet sauce coating the pears. Add the agave or sweetener of choice once pears are finished coking.
6. Put mixture in a container and refrigerate until completely cool.
7. In a mixing bowl, add the yogurt and fold in the pear mixture.
8. Enjoy plain or serve with granola.

Note:
Keeps in the refrigerator for up to one week. Stir well before consuming.

Lemon Yogurt

Zesty, fresh, sweet, and full of vitamin C, lemon yogurt is easy, healthful, and a winner for just about everyone, including children! The creamy, smooth consistency makes this a wonderful go-to yogurt for those who don't like the texture of pulp from added fruit.

Adding lemon yogurt to smoothies is brilliant! It gives the smoothie a subtle refreshing zest, which helps bring forward the flavors of the other fruit. Try the Strawberry Mango smoothie (page 205) using lemon yogurt or make a parfait with homemade granola and clementines.

Ingredients:

For 1 quart:

- 1 quart whole milk or Greek yogurt (page 179 or 181)
- 2 tablespoons fresh lemon juice
- Zest of one whole lemon
- ¼ to ⅓ cup agave nectar

Instructions:

1. In a small bowl, whisk together lemon juice, lemon zest, and agave nectar.
2. Pour into a jar or bowl with the yogurt and mix until combined.

Note:
Keeps in the refrigerator for up to two weeks.

Smoothies

About Smoothies

Smoothies are a fun and tasty way of getting probiotics, vitamins, and minerals into our systems. Endless flavors and textures can be concocted to whip up a healthful breakfast smoothie, snack, or even dessert. Smoothies don't have to be limited to fruit and yogurt. They can also easily include raw nuts, nut butters, coconut, soy or almond milks, coffee, spices, extracts (such as vanilla or almond), vegetables and more!

I find that the best smoothies are the result of using fresh, in-season ripe fruit that has been frozen. While grocery stores carry frozen fruit, the selection is very limited when taking into account the wide array of fresh fruits available. Oftentimes, store-bought frozen fruit includes fruit that was picked before it ripened, which can result in an overly-tart or bland smoothie. Purchasing in-season ripe fruit, chopping it, then freezing it, ensures sweet, delicious, healthful smoothies can be made year-round.

Thick, cold, sweet, and creamy smoothies are my favorite! For this reason, I buy bunches of bananas, let them get very ripe, then peel and freeze them so that I can make a tasty smoothie any time I wish. Frozen bananas do wonders for making smoothies naturally sweet, keeping them cold longer, and giving them a creamy consistency. It doesn't take much time to fill a freezer-safe container with ripe bananas, but the payoff is glorious! If you have a sweet tooth like me, you can also use chopped dates or figs to add extra sweetness to your smoothies.

Using a high-powered blender is a steadfast way of achieving a smoothie that is uniform in consistency. For those who do not own a powerful blender, never fear! Simply add the liquids (milks, juices, yogurt, or kefir) in the blender first, followed by the soft fruit, then hard frozen fruit. This enables the blender to process the smoothie more efficiently and smoothly.

This section includes smoothies that are both yogurt and kefir-based. Most of the smoothies are made using yogurt and kefir recipes out of this very book! In each recipe, I provide options for various store-bought or homemade yogurt flavors that can be used.

Have you tried a green smoothie? How about a smoothie with coconut milk? What about a smoothie with roasted beets? You will find all sorts of flavor profiles in this section, using fruits, vegetables, and even chocolate to quench your every craving any time of year.

Strawberry Mango Smoothie

This simple fruit smoothie is packed with flavor. It has been my go-to smoothie every since I was a teenager and it never fails! The sweet, creamy, zesty, tart flavors are perfectly balanced and all the fruit used is easy to find year-round. For this smoothie, I used homemade lemon yogurt (page 201), but you can also purchase yogurt from the grocery store.

Ingredients:

- 1 cup lemon yogurt (page 201)
- ¾ cup unsweetened almond milk
- 6 ripe strawberries (fresh or frozen)
- 1 frozen banana
- 1 whole mango, peeled, chopped, and frozen

Instructions:

Add all ingredients to a blender and blend until smooth.

Note:
If you are not using a high-powered blender, be sure to put the yogurt and almond milk in first. You can also add additional almond milk to help the blender process all of the fruit.

Makes a thick smoothie for two people!

Tropical Green Smoothie

Green smoothies don't have to taste green. They can taste tropical, refreshing, and delicious! This smoothie is packed with island flavor and is a wonderful introduction to green smoothies for those who are new to them. Besides tasting great, pineapples have many health benefits. They are high in vitamin C, are a natural anti-inflammatory, and due to their acidity, they help prevent bacteria growth in the mouth. Couple these benefits with the antioxidants and high vitamin K and vitamin A content of kale and you've got yourself an immune-boosting powerhouse smoothie!

While this recipe calls for roasted banana kefir (page 171), you can easily replace this with one cup of plain kefir and throw in a frozen banana.

Ingredients:

- 2 cups fresh pineapple, chopped
- 1 whole mango, chopped and frozen (about 2 cups)
- 1 cup roasted banana kefir* (page 171)
- 1 cup almond milk
- 2 cups kale leaves, lightly packed

*The roasted banana kefir can be replaced with 1 cup of plain kefir plus one whole frozen banana

Instructions:

In a high powered blender, add all the ingredients and blend until completely smooth. This makes a thick smoothie, so you may need to stop the blender, stir the ingredients around, and restart it. For a thinner smoothie, add additional almond milk and/or kefir.

Makes smoothies for 2 to 3 people

Peaches 'n' Cream ('n' Honey) Smoothie

There is nothing but simple peachy goodness all wrapped up in this recipe! Using Peach & Honey Kefir (page 167) plus 1 frozen peach and some almond milk, you have yourself an easy, creamy, sweet, peachy treat. But don't worry if you don't have any homemade peach kefir on hand! You can simply replace it with one cup of plain kefir plus an additional peach and some honey.

During peach season, I stock up. I like to buy pounds of peaches, allow them to ripen (if they aren't already), chop them up, and freeze them so that I can enjoy them year-round. Unfortunately, peach season seems to be way too short, so when juicy ripe peaches are available during the summer, I'm always sure to get my fill!

Ingredients:

- 1 peach, pitted, chopped, and frozen
- 1 cup peach & honey kefir (page 167)*
- ½ cup almond milk

Instructions:

Add all ingredients to a blender and blend until smooth.

Note:
**You can replace the Peach & Honey Kefir with 1 cup plain kefir plus an additional frozen peach and 1 tablespoon of honey*

Makes 1 large smoothie

Chocolate Protein Smoothie

If there is one food item that never lasts long in my house, it's a jar of peanut butter. Crunchy or creamy, it doesn't matter to me as long as I can scoop it with a spoon! I prefer the all natural nut butters that have no added oils, sugars, or preservatives and have found that although most nut butters taste great in a smoothie, peanut butter is still my favorite.

This smoothie includes raw cacao powder, which is chocolate in its raw form before it has been heat treated and had oils or sugars added to it. The cacao powder can be replaced with regular cocoa powder but there is a slight difference in flavor. I also include maca powder in this smoothie, which is optional but very healthful. Maca powder comes from maca roots, which are typically grown in Peru. It is full of vitamins B1, B2, B12, C, and E and also mineral rich. It is an aphrodisiac, can help increase the stamina of athletes, and also helps to restore red blood cells, making it a heart-healthy food.

I have tried this smoothie with a variety of yogurts and kefir. My favorites are chocolate kefir, mocha yogurt, and vanilla yogurt. Although all these options are delicious, the smoothie is also great without yogurt.

Ingredients:

- 1 frozen banana
- ½ cup chocolate kefir, mocha yogurt, or vanilla yogurt (page 165, 189, or 191)
- ½ to ¾ cup almond milk*
- 1½ tablespoons your favorite peanut butter**
- 1½ tablespoons raw cacao powder
- ½ teaspoon raw maca powder, optional

Instructions:

Place all ingredients in a blender and blend until smooth.

Note:
**For an extra rich and decadent treat, try using dark chocolate almond milk!*
***Also try this smoothie using cashew butter or almond butter!*

Makes 1 smoothie

Raspberry Piña Colada Smoothie

Piña Coladas are the quintessential island vacation beverage and for a very good reason: they're sweet and creamy and something about them says relaxation. I adapted the boozy beverage to be a smoothie that can be enjoyed any time of day. It includes full-fat coconut milk, making it a rich smoothie full of health benefits. Although coconut milk is high in calories, it is full of heart-healthy fats that will not clog arteries. It also contains vitamins B, C, and E, minerals, and antioxidants. Coconut is also known to boost metabolism. While you can easily use fresh pineapple for this smoothie, I prefer using pineapple juice because it creates a creamy texture. Pineapple juice is also great for you, as it is full of vitamins C and B6, antioxidants, and is an energy booster and digestive aid.

Raspberries are chock-full of antioxidants and vitamin C, and they are a natural anti-inflammatory. They also contain rheosmin, which helps fats that you consume to pass through the system without being absorbed, making them an anti-obesity food. All these benefits combined make this seemingly decadent treat great for you!

I mashed up fresh raspberries for this recipe and added them in the smoothie after I blended the other ingredients, which gives the smoothie a nice tart flavor and some texture. You are free to leave the raspberries out altogether if you're looking for a completely smooth beverage.

Ingredients:

- ½ cup plain yogurt* (page 179)
- ½ cup coconut milk**
- ½ cup pineapple juice
- 1½ frozen bananas
- ½ cup fresh raspberries, mashed

*Also consider using banana cream pie yogurt or vanilla yogurt
**I recommend using full-fat coconut milk from the can. This smoothie will not be as delicious without it!

Instructions:

1. Place the fresh raspberries in a bowl and mash them using a fork. Set aside.

2. Add the plain yogurt, coconut milk, pineapple juice, and frozen banana to a blender and blend until completely smooth.

3. Pour the smoothie into a glass and drop in the mashed raspberries. Enjoy!

Blueberry Mango Smoothie

This packed-full-of-fruit smoothie is a definite crowd pleaser. It is very easy to throw together when you're pinched for time and it has a something-for-everyone flavor. Children will especially love this tasty treat! I love to layer smoothies by adding either coconut milk or yogurt on top. This not only gives the smoothie a unique and pretty look, but also makes a treat that can either be mixed together or enjoyed layer by layer.

Adding blueberry kefir or blueberry yogurt to the smoothie PLUS a whole cup of blueberries makes for a drink rich in antioxidants. Blueberries are known as a brain food and studies show they help improve memory. Whenever I studied for finals, I was sure to drink blueberry smoothies leading up to my exams. Add in the mango, orange juice, and banana, and you have a flavor-filled drink that's full of immune-boosting vitamins and minerals!

Ingredients:

- 1 whole mango, peeled, pitted, chopped, and frozen
- 1 cup frozen blueberries
- 1 ripe banana, frozen
- ½ cup blueberry kefir or blueberry yogurt* (page 173 or 193)
- ½ cup almond milk
- ½ cup orange juice
- ¼ to ½ cup full-fat coconut milk (for topping)

Instructions:

1. Add all ingredients except for the coconut milk to a blender. Blend until completely smooth.
2. Pour the smoothie into two glasses and serve with coconut milk floater on top.

Note:
**Blueberry kefir or yogurt can be replaced with other favorite yogurt, such as vanilla, strawberry, or raspberry.*

Makes a smoothie for two!

Chocolate Beetroot Smoothie

It may seem odd to blend cacao powder, beets, and cranberry kefir together, but this is my favorite smoothie. There are so many powerful health qualities to this smoothie, we should all be drinking one every day! I will give a fair warning that this smoothie is not palatable for just anyone and everyone. You can, indeed, taste the beets (although the cranberry and chocolate flavor come through more), so those folks who have a strong distaste for beets may not enjoy this smoothie.

This smoothie is filled with a great deal of vitamins, minerals, and antioxidants. Chocolate is very rich in antioxidants and cacao contains phenylethylamine, which stimulates the adrenal system to speed your heart rate and make you feel happy and alert. Beets are full of fiber and the sugars are slow-burning, making them a healthy source of carbohydrates. Beets also contain nitrates, which help expand the walls of your blood vessels, giving you more energy and brain power! Not to mention, they're a natural aphrodisiac. All of this on top of the vitamin C and antioxidants in cranberries makes this smoothie an all-around winner!

Ingredients:

- ½ red beet, steamed, chopped, and frozen
- 1½ tablespoons raw cacao powder (or regular cocoa powder)
- 1 frozen banana
- ½ cup cranberry kefir (page 163)
- ½ cup almond milk*

Instructions:

1. Fill a pot with 2 inches of water, insert your steamer, and bring the water to a boil.
2. Chop one whole beet into quarters, leaving the peel on, place it in the pot, and cover the pot.
3. Steam the beet for 15 minutes or until it is soft when poked with a fork.
4. Allow the beet to cool completely. Once cool, chop it into smaller pieces and freeze it in a freezer-safe container. Since you only need half the beet, you can use the other half in a salad or freeze it for another smoothie.
5. Add all ingredients to a blender and blend until completely smooth.

Note:
If you don't have a steamer, you can also place the beet directly in boiling water (or even roast it) to cook it.

Makes one smoothie

Cantaloupe Mint Cooler

Layered smoothies are lots of fun and are pretty to look at as well as delicious. Instead of blending everything together, floating the yogurt on top makes for a unique treat. When frozen then blended, cantaloupe has a similar texture to a slushy. The fresh mint and cantaloupe together make for a delicious, refreshing drink on a hot day!

This cooler calls for the Mojito Yogurt from the yogurt section of this book (page 187). You can also use the Key Lime Kefir, Lemon Yogurt, or Vanilla Yogurt

Ingredients:

- 1 whole cantaloupe, seeded, chopped, and frozen
- 6 mint leaves
- 1 tablespoon fresh lime juice
- 1 cup almond milk
- 1 tablespoon agave (optional)
- 1 cup Mojito Yogurt (page 187)*

*Try this recipe with key lime kefir or lemon yogurt! Even vanilla yogurt tastes great atop this cooler!

Instructions:

1. Chop the cantaloupe into chunks, discarding the rind. Place the chunks in a freezer-safe container and freeze. (Note: You can also skip this step but frozen cantaloupe makes a refreshing slushy.)

2. Add all of the ingredients except for the yogurt to a blender.

3. Blend until a thick slushy results. Depending on how powerful your blender is, you may have to stop it, mix the cantaloupe around, and continue to blend several times. If you don't have a high-power blender, I suggest using fresh cantaloupe instead of frozen.

4. Pour cantaloupe cooler into two glasses and distribute half of the yogurt atop each cooler. You can mix in the yogurt for a nice creamy treat or enjoy the layers separately with a spoon.

Matcha Green Tea Smoothie

Green tea is one of the best sources for antioxidants. While brewing a hot cup of green tea is great for you, most of the health benefits of green tea remain trapped in the tea leaves, which get discarded with the used tea bag. Matcha powder is stone-ground green tea leaves (it's what is used in green tea ice cream!) and is a powerful source of antioxidants, vitamins, minerals, and amino acids. Matcha also boosts metabolism and burns fat.

It doesn't take very much matcha to make a tasty and healthful smoothie. The flavor of green tea is subtle, so using neutral fruit, such as bananas or mangoes, in a green tea smoothie prevents the flavor from getting lost. This healthy drink will boost your immune system, give you energy, and is tasty to boot!

Ingredients:

- 1½ frozen bananas*
- ¾ cup vanilla yogurt (page 191)
- 1 cup almond milk
- 1 to 2 teaspoons matcha green tea powder

*Also try a Mango Matcha smoothie using a frozen chopped mango (about 1½ to 2 cups frozen mango)

Instructions:

Add all ingredients to a blender and blend until smooth.

Makes 1 large or 2 small smoothies

Mojito Smoothie

One of the most refreshing summertime cocktails is the mint mojito. This mojito-inspired smoothie incorporates lime and mint for a cool, zesty flavor, and also coconut milk and kefir for a decadent, creamy treat. Although this is not a low-calorie smoothie, it is full of health benefits from the probiotic-rich kefir and electrolyte-filled coconut milk. Drink this after a long jog on a hot day for a rejuvenating beverage or enjoy for dessert!

Ingredients:

- 2 ripe frozen bananas
- 12 fresh mint leaves
- ½ cup key lime kefir (page 161)*
- ½ cup coconut milk (full-fat from the can)
- ½ cup almond milk

*Key Lime Kefir can be replaced with ½ cup plain kefir + 1 tablespoon fresh lime juice + 1 tablespoon agave nectar

Instructions:

Add everything to a blender and blend until smooth.

Makes smoothies for two!

Avocado Kale Superfood Smoothie

This smoothie is truly a meal in a glass. It contains blueberries, kale, and avocado, which are all very healthful foods. Blueberries are rich in antioxidants and kale is dense in iron, fiber, vitamins K and A, and much more. Avocados contain healthy omega-3 fatty acids and has been said to prevent Alzheimer's, cancer, and heart disease. Avocados also have a wide array of vitamins and minerals. When all's said and done, this cup of smoothie has everything you need for a healthful meal!

The pillow-y texture of this smoothie gives it a blissful mouth feel. It is sweet and creamy and slightly earthy. It may not be a favorite of those who are new to green smoothies, but it is also definitely not the kind of green drink that makes you hold your nose!

Ingredients:

- 1 frozen banana, chopped in small chunks
- ½ cup blueberry yogurt (page 193)
- 1 cup kale (or spinach leaves) leaves, chopped
- ½ ripe avocado
- ½ cup unsweetened almond milk

Instructions:

Add all ingredients to a blender and blend until completely smooth

Note:
A high-powered blender is recommended for this smoothie because it turns out thick and creamy. For a thinner consistency or to help the blender to process all of the ingredients, add additional almond milk.

Makes 1 thick smoothie

Turmeric Kefir Lassi

A lassi is a yogurt-based beverage that does not have to contain fruit. It is similar to a smoothie and can sometimes include various spices and even salt. Each ingredient in this drink is incredibly healthy in its own unique way, giving this beverage a high density and large array of health benefits.

Turmeric has been touted as a great tool for preventing cancer cell growth. It is also an anti-inflammatory, which helps ease skin ailments such as psoriasis. Turmeric has been known to slow the progression of Alzheimer's, is an antioxidant, and is also a natural pain killer. Similar to turmeric, ginger is an anti-inflammatory and is known to be a digestive aid, ease nausea and menstrual cramps, and is a natural antibiotic.

Honey is a natural antibiotic. Couple all these fun facts with the vitamins, minerals, immunity, and metabolism boosting qualities of fresh pineapple and coconut milk (not to mention the probiotics in the kefir), and this smoothie should be at the top of the list to make!

Now that you know the benefits, what does this thing taste like? It's creamy and sweet with brilliant texture. The two dominant flavors you get are the lemon and the ginger. Lemon and ginger together produce a creamy flavor, so the beverage is all-around delicious!

Ingredients:

- 1 cup plain milk kefir* (page 152–15)
- 1 frozen banana
- ½ cup fresh pineapple
- ¼ cup coconut milk
- ½ lemon, juiced
- 1 heaping teaspoon fresh ginger, grated on the fine side of a box grater
- 1 teaspoon turmeric
- 1 household teaspoon honey**

*Plain kefir can be substituted for plain yogurt
**Note the difference between a household teaspoon and a regular teaspoon. A household teaspoon is literally the spoon you would use to stir tea and holds slightly more than a measuring teaspoon.

Instructions:

1. Finely grate a piece of peeled ginger root using the fine side of a box grater until you have 1 heaping teaspoon. The amount of ginger can be scaled up if you like additional spice.
2. Add all ingredients to a blender and blend until smooth.
3. Pour smoothie in a glass and garnish with additional turmeric.

Pumpkin Spice Smoothie

During the fall and winter, there's something so comforting about pumpkin, cinnamon, and ginger. Pumpkin treats are fun, delicious, and can actually be very healthful! Pumpkins are very high in vitamin A, fiber, and are low in fat and calories. Combined with fresh ginger and cinnamon, this treat is sure to kick your sweet tooth, satisfy your hunger, and provide you a healthy alternative to dessert.

Did you know ginger is a natural inflammatory and aids in digestion while cinnamon helps regulate blood sugar? These warm spices are great for your body and are especially satisfying on a cold autumn or winter day. The recipe calls for pumpkin purée, which can either be purchased in a can from the store, or you can use purée from roasting a pumpkin at home.

Ingredients:

- ½ cup pumpkin purée (or sweet potato purée)
- ½ cup plain yogurt (or maple yogurt) (page 179)
- ½ cup unsweetened almond milk
- 1 frozen banana
- 1 heaping teaspoon honey
- ¼ teaspoon ground cinnamon
- ½ teaspoon fresh ginger, grated
- Pinch nutmeg

Instructions:

1. Using the fine side of a box grater, finely grate a small piece of peeled ginger root until you have about ½ teaspoon.
2. Add all ingredients to a blender and blend until smooth!

Note:
If you do not have a high powered blender, add a little more almond milk to help blend everything up.

Makes 1 thick smoothie

About the Author:

"I began brewing kombucha in 2011, soon after I discovered it at the grocery store. While it took me a couple of bottles to acquire a taste for kombucha, I fell in love with the way it made me feel and, soon after, fell in love with the flavor as well. I began buying and drinking a bottle every day, which got expensive quickly. Put bluntly, I realized how much money I was spending each month on my kombucha fixation and figured there must be a better way!

I knew making kombucha at home would not only be a fun project, but it would save me money and, ultimately, I would have control over the ingredients that went into the process. When I first started brewing kombucha, I flavored it using 100 percent fruit juices only. Once I began using fruit and herbs to flavor kombucha during secondary fermentation, my entire kombucha world flipped upside down in a very positive way. Not only did my kombucha taste better, but it also became fizzier and I was able to cater to my nutritional needs by adding ingredients containing specific vitamins, minerals, and the health benefits I was seeking.

I am not a nutritionist or dietitian, nor do I have any formal education in health sciences whatsoever. All of the information in this book has come from my own research and experience. I have had many triumphs and failures. The more I experiment, the more I learn. Throughout this book, I share what has worked and not worked for me in the beautiful art of fermentation.

I do not have any digestive conditions that led me to seek out probiotic sources, but I believe having probiotics in my diet helps make my holy temple a happy home. For those of you who do have digestive conditions, probiotics are a great way to help heal your body, but please do not rely solely on this book for your nutritional awareness.

While I love brewing probiotic beverages, I am utterly passionate about cooking and photography. I write a food blog called The Roasted Root *(http://www.theroastedroot.net), where I share nutrient-dense recipes that are primarily focused on whole foods. I develop recipes based on seasonal ingredients and my own nutritional needs. I photograph the end result, then post the recipe and photos along with my thoughts, feelings, and general banter on my blog. Not only does my blog provide me a wonderful creative outlet, but it has also opened up doors in a way I never anticipated. The future holds meaningful relationships, healthy food, and delicious probiotics. I welcome you to share these experiences with me!"*

Index

Conversion Charts

Metric and Imperial Conversions

(These conversions are rounded for convenience)

Ingredient	Cups/ Tablespoons/ Teaspoons	Ounces	Grams/ Milliliters
Fruit, dried	1 cup	4 ounces	120 grams
Fruits or veggies, chopped	1 cup	5 to 7 ounces	145 to 200 grams
Fruits or veggies, puréed	1 cup	8.5 ounces	245 grams
Honey, maple syrup, or corn syrup	1 tablespoon	0.75 ounce	20 grams
Liquids: cream, milk, water, or juice	1 cup	8 fluid ounces	240 milliliters
Salt	1 teaspoon	0.2 ounces	6 grams
Spices: cinnamon, cloves, ginger, or nutmeg (ground)	1 teaspoon	0.2 ounce	5 milliliters
Sugar, brown, firmly packed	1 cup	7 ounces	200 grams
Sugar, white	1 cup/ 1 tablespoon	7 ounces/0.5 ounce	200 grams/12.5 grams
Vanilla extract	1 teaspoon	0.2 ounce	4 grams

Liquids

8 fluid ounces = 1 cup = ½ pint
16 fluid ounces = 2 cups = 1 pint
32 fluid ounces = 4 cups = 1 quart
128 fluid ounces = 16 cups = 1 gallon

RECIPE NOTES

RECIPE NOTES

RECIPE NOTES

RECIPE NOTES